Smile because it happened

Smile because it happened

Antidotes to melancholy in Thailand, the land of smiles

PATRICK FORSYTH

R3THINK PRESS

First Published in Great Britain 2013
by Rethink Press (www.rethinkpress.com)

© Copyright Patrick Forsyth

All rights reserved. No part of this publication may be reproduced, stored in or introduced into a retrieval system, or transmitted, in any form, or by any means (electronic, mechanical, photocopying, recording or otherwise) without the prior written permission of the publisher.

This book is sold subject to the condition that it shall not, by way of trade or otherwise, be lent, resold, hired out, or otherwise circulated without the publisher's prior consent in any form of binding or cover other than that in which it is published and without a similar condition including this condition being imposed on the subsequent purchaser.

Cover image © www.istockphoto.com/hypnattize

For Siripan, Silvia and Jack –
all a major part of my love affair with Thailand

"Don't cry because it's over, smile because it happened."
Dr Seuss

AUTHOR'S NOTE

Both my previous travel books have recorded discreet journeys. In the case of *First Class At Last!* it was a train journey from Singapore, through Malaysia and into Thailand; in *Beguiling Burma* it was a river journey through Burma. This time I am concerned not with one journey, but with one country and a miscellany of experiences from many visits.

My first trip to Thailand was more than 25 years ago. It was the first Eastern place I had been to – my main destination was Singapore, where I had business – and it all seemed very exotic. It was also unbelievably inexpensive, the exchange rate getting you more than twice what it does now. Tourism was nowhere near as developed as now and one felt, if not quite a pioneer, then at least one of a minority and unusually privileged to be experiencing it. I have returned many times since, on both business and pleasure, and acquired a great affection for the country, the culture and the people.

This book tells why. Thailand is not just a place for a nice holiday, though it is a marvellous holiday destination; it is a place where everything about it, the people, the sights, sounds and the way things are done, all combine to captivate you. It would surely take a real effort of will not to become a regular visitor.

This does not aim to be a guide book, though places of interest are mentioned, rather here are some miscellaneous jottings about my experiences in the land of smiles; they aim to show why the place is so special and why, above all, so much about it always brings a smile to my face.

Note: the Thai currency is the *baht,* as I write around 50 to one pound sterling.

CONTENTS

Prelude   1

1. Request Considered: Audience Granted   15
2. The Elephants' Smile   29
3. What's In Store?   39
4. A Little Luxury   57
5. Floating Away Your Worries   69
6. Don't Hold Your Breath   81
7. So Sorry, We're Closed   95
8. Friend Indeed   115
9. Amongst The Ruins   131
10. Plans In A Cold Climate   147
11. Transport Of Delight   155
12. Eating, Raining, Feeting   167
13. Making Tracks   191
14. An Arresting Experience   217

PRELUDE

*"He used to be depressed and miserable.
Now he's miserable and depressed."*
Bowie Kuhn

Whoever the quotation above referred to, it could apply to a good many people. Even though I like to think that I am essentially a happy, optimistic and contented sort of person, and believe being so is the best way to enjoy life, the number of seemingly miserable people you can cross paths with in a single day can have you wondering if they know something that you don't. Would it hurt some of them to crack a smile? Smiling has a contagion to it and really can, as the song has it, spread a little happiness. Indeed one country, Thailand, is known as the land of smiles and this is for, as we will see, good reason.

But the truth is that many people do seem to be miserable and that a surfeit of them can see even the most optimistic of us experiencing just a little bit of a dent in our contentment. As chance would have it, I began writing this on 22nd January, a date that no less a source than Britain's *Sun* newspaper officially nominates as the "most likely day in the year to make you feel miserable" day. Even their perkiest page three girl evidently cannot relieve the doom and gloom of this particular morning. How do they know, I wonder?

My day went well enough and even a minor computer glitch failed to dent my *bonhomie*, but misery and discontent do seem to be a common malaise. A survey reported by the BBC, surely a slightly more reliable source than the *Sun* newspaper, says that one in three British people feels "downright miserable", though quite where that sits on whatever overall scale of things that implies was not explained: somewhere between "Wow, I'm just ecstatic" and "Where do I sign up for euthanasia?" perhaps. It gets worse: one in ten Brits evidently feel that they have been dealt a miserable lot, are powerless to alter it and would be better off dead. One in ten! Ten in a hundred! That must mean that if you walk down a busy street you pass a potential suicide every few metres; I must buy a few shares in an undertaking business.

The survey also reported that many people hate their work, and feel "exhausted, unappreciated or underpaid". Furthermore – and here's a truly epic revelation – fully a quarter of those people interviewed said that they felt life was "unfair". What's that? Life's unfair! The perception and insight of these people simply astounds! Of course life is unfair: wholly, completely, utterly, irrevocably and always unfair. What else? Perhaps it is vainly expecting it *not* to be unfair that makes some people despair. At least pessimists are either never disappointed or able to say "I told you so" on a regular basis, as they tick off their gloomy predictions; this gives them two options, either of which should cheer them up, but apparently doesn't.

As I've said, I do not put myself in this particular camp, but those who do seem to do their best to spread their misery about and bring their happier brethren down to their level. Maybe they think that passing it on helps them: perhaps they believe that if they offload a dollop of their melancholy someone else, their own burden will become that much less.

Or maybe actually wanting to depress others just goes with being of an unsmiling disposition.

Sometimes one seems to get more than one's fair share of exposure to such people. Recently my broadband connection was more off than on for two months. Having run the gauntlet of their multilayered telephone system – *"Please select from the following options..."* – I must have spoken to 20 or 30 people at my service provider, and every single one of them seemed to be having a bad day. Not so, people of my service provider (Orange, actually, they put me through too much for me not to name and shame them)! No, it was *me* having a bad two months and your job was to fix it, not to moan about the system and apply the fine detail of your bureaucracy in a way that made matters worse. For instance, which unthinking brain-dead idiot within your labyrinthine organisation thought it was a good idea to email me when you knew my problem was no broadband and... surprise, surprise... no email? Apart from the general unhelpfulness, lies and avoidance of responsibility during so many of these calls, it really does not help to add what are intended to be pleasantries and are manifestly not, like reading "Thank you for calling Orange" off the card after I have hung on for 25 minutes and got nowhere... again. Or telling me that recording my call will help provide "excellent service". It. Does. Not. I was on the telephone to all these people, of course, but I bet that if I could have seen them there would not have been a hint of a smile amongst the whole blooming lot of them – shame on you all. Sorry, just occasionally my life is not all sweetness and light.

On the other hand, when I caught a bus in London the other day, one of the old style ones that have a conductor to collect the fares, the guy was happiness personified. He was "selling" destinations. When I asked for a ticket to Pentonville Road, he immediately suggested I went further on: to Islington. "Nice place that," he said encouragingly, "you can walk along the canal. Go on, it only costs a little more." This banter went on for some time and was repeated in various forms to other passengers as more boarded. He smiled, indeed he beamed. Everyone else smiled back – some people even lowered their reserve enough to smile at each other about it – and the journey passed very pleasantly, though I resolutely stuck to my guns and alighted at Pentonville Road. When I did, he still smiled and wished me well. So expressing an outwardly contented demeanour can be done, and I would hazard a guess that, not least, that bus conductor did it because it made his task easier and more fun. It certainly seemed to be appreciated by his passengers.

Yet, that particular bus apart, travel can be an area of unrelieved gloom. The people who staff airports are not, for the most part, high on any smile-ometer rating, certainly not in Britain. London's Heathrow recently won the award for supplying the worst personal experience short of amputating your own finger with a mincing machine. Actually, of course, I made that up, but it certainly deserves it and is responsible for one very particular kind of terminal illness. It is dreary, unpleasant and when the doors on an arriving plane finally open (no one in authority, it seems, ever actually expects arrivals; certainly it often takes 20 minutes once the plane has stopped for people to realise that passengers need to disembark and allow the doors to open), the last thing you are going to see is a smile. Recently things have got so bad that the government is trying to make airport operator

British Airports Authority sell some of its many airports to break up its monopoly and create a bit of competition designed to prompt some good service. I won't hold my breath. BAA is owned by a Spanish company and will doubtless reply "Manyana" and continue to busy itself counting the profit from the sale of duty free goods while ordinary passengers continue to suffer.

Be that as it may, you must deal with numbers of staff as you make your way through an airport. At the check-in desk, if they smile they do so with the kind of look that disguises their "I'm feeling like if I have to be polite to one more passenger, I shall scream" demeanour, though the disguise is usually poor. At security they rarely smile at all as notices above them describe how you will be prosecuted if you should even think about being nasty to them. It is a sign of the times that such notices are necessary; what have the rude minority got against people who are only there to stop you crashing to earth from 30,000 feet in a bomb-induced fireball, I wonder? I am happy to have all the security seen as useful, thanks very much.

The crowds and queues elsewhere in airports do not encourage pleasant transactions with anyone else to whom you may need to speak; indeed my advice is to avoid doing so. Books, magazines and the now ubiquitous iPod are the best defence and provide a way of separating you to a degree from the whole grizzly business, at least mentally. Checked in for a visit to the land of smiles (just to get me in the mood for writing this) and a flight to Bangkok, I am on my way to the Thai lounge. The airline's slogan is "Smooth as silk", so I should be assured of an above average reception there, a veritable antidote to this prevailing culture of apparent misery. And indeed I am: even though the lady behind the check-in counter was not Thai, her smile of welcome seemed genuine and actually seemed to indicate that the person smiling was content with her lot. There was a Thai lady on duty in the lounge and she smiled beautifully.

So to the plane: the airlines are always at pains to tell us how wonderful the experience of flying is. Flight announcements as you set off always end with the words, *Enjoy your flight*, and, though some airlines have the good grace to say that they "hope" you enjoy it, so many things conspire to render this about as likely as winning the lottery that the words never ring true. After all how can several hours crushed in a tiny seat inside a metal tube, being dehydrated, watching a cut-down version of a film of which the best review said "dire" and eating dinner at breakfast time, be in any small way pleasurable?

You have a significant choice when you make a flight booking. Will you turn right or left as you enter the plane? Bearing in mind that on long haul flights you need a mortgage (if you can get one) to fly economy, and that business class needs a budget like the GNP of a small country, the choice may very well be made for you. Escalating taxes in the UK compound the problem. If financially you can run to the upper classes it certainly helps a tad, but even then there is one obstacle to a smooth flight that is difficult to control.

What's that?

It is who sits next to you. Think about it. Half the population seem to make unpleasant travelling companions: the overweight, intoxicated, and those with verbal diarrhoea or flatulence; also insomniacs, fidgets, babies and small unruly children, and many more. Watch the scene in any airport lounge. No one makes goo-goo eyes at babies or pulls faces at other people's children, especially in these days of reducing parental discipline. They just hope some kind of seat selection god exists and pray silently for any obnoxious ankle biter to be at the other end of the plane from them or, better still, left behind. Perhaps the airlines could clamp down a little: *I am sorry Mrs Stephens, but your baby is too noisy and will have to be checked into the hold.* Go on: Ryanair at least might do this, though they might also charge everyone else a child-free-flight-supplement. I once saw a sign in an airport saying simply "Parents' Room"; maybe it was so that even parents could hide away as their children roamed the airport wreaking havoc.

Some fellow passengers are bizarre: odd ones I have encountered include a terrified undertaker and an unaccompanied six year old who told me her mother could not come because – "she's like dead". Perhaps I should have investigated, but I didn't. Others are informative, like an off duty pilot I once had sitting alongside me who explained that landing a plane is easy – "All you have to do is to slow it down to a speed at which the plane will not fly any more, and drops out of the sky like a stone. The trick is to be a foot off the ground when that happens." I have never been sure whether to be reassured by this or terrified.

Given the volume of travellers, guaranteeing that the seat next to you will be empty is well nigh impossible. On anything but budget airlines, where you need to wear running shoes as you go on board to ensure getting any space at all, seats are pre-allocated. Tactics that work on a bus, say, cannot apply. On a bus, incidentally, it is no good putting bags down to block the seat beside you, the kind of person you want to discourage will take a perverse pleasure in asking you to move them. Better to pat the seat next to you and give them a maniacal smile; no one wants to sit next to the nutter. Nor, back to planes, can you guarantee that a gorgeous, doe-eyed nymphomaniac who unaccountably fancies you to bits and is intent on joining the mile-high club will occupy the seat next to you. Still less can you guarantee that it will not be occupied by a stressed mother whose fractious two-year old screams without pause and wholly unchecked throughout the entire flight, and who asks you to hold things for her as she changes nappies.

But one man has set out to help with all this.

Following in the footsteps of websites like Friends Reunited, American Peter Shankman has set up the site airtroductions.com. This allows you to register your personal details alongside details of any flight you plan to take and to set out details, too, of what kind of person you would like to sit next to you. The success of this is dependent, of course, on someone else who is both on your flight and logs onto the same site actually liking the sound of your details and requesting to sit next to you. Or on you succeeding in locating someone who suits you. It must make for some odd requests: *Nervous first time flyer, non-smoker, seeks more experienced neighbour for handholding and maybe more.* Or: *Experienced jetsetter seeks to join mile high club with like-minded soul with good stamina and high boredom threshold.* Actually, it is a form of what is now popularly known as networking and the site's proud founder is quoted as saying, "We all fly so much, I thought there must be a better way to use all that time in the air. I have sat next to chief executives, marketing directors and movie stars. The discussions have led to gaining new clients, lots of business and even a date or two."

For the most part I have rarely ever sat next to anyone on an aircraft who did not disturb me in some way or another or bore me silly if we got talking. So I find the thought of sitting next to some weird web-surfing traveller, who not only thinks that this form of travel-companion finding is a neat idea, but who also actually pays (yes, there's a charge!) to register with it, really very scary. Even the nutter on the bus is not usually that worrying. So I have resolved to take my chances and so far declined to log on and add my name to the list. In any case, what would I say? Maybe: *Cynical traveller seeks slim, sober travel companion wanting to sleep through the entire flight; will provide sleeping pill.* Or: *Is anyone out there booked on my flight, and has a family emergency that will prevent them from travelling? May I have your unoccupied seat next to me please?*

Enough. They are calling my flight. Fingers crossed. Maybe at last I am due some serendipity even though I am turning right – or maybe I will sit with that six-year old again. Perhaps the only real solution is to take a nice companion with you. This time my luck is in: after crossing everything in sight for the duration of embarkation, the doors close and the seat next to me remains pleasingly empty. I am by the window. The aisle seat is taken by an inoffensive looking woman. We exchange only a brief greeting, but exchange smiles that both say, "What a stroke of luck". After all the hassle of the airport it makes a happy start. One of the stewardesses observes us acknowledging the situation and smiles too, more than a welcoming smile, one apparently joining in our pleasure. That's the second nice Thai smile today. What is it the old song says? "If you just smile..." It makes a difference; so much so that there is actually a world smile capital.

In the USA, if you go to Idaho you will find Pocatello, a small town of not much more than 50,000 people, named after a 19th century Shoshone chieftain. Once it was an important trading stop on the Oregon Trail and a place that developed when the gold rush of the mid 1800s brought many settlers to the region. I have not been there, but these days it appears in most respects to be an unremarkable town, though it is home to Idaho State University. Its one claim to fame is that it is known as America's Smile Capital, something that seems perhaps to make it worth a visit, though it has this description only because it once had a curious local bylaw that forbade people looking miserable; it was actually against the law *not* to smile. My goodness, that would get a few prosecutions underway in London's rush hour – a time when almost everyone looks dejected or surly. Now the law is no more and the town probably has a normal measure of misery guts just like everywhere else, but it still holds an annual Smile Fest to remember the old law. The trouble is that the process of travelling there over any distance would almost certainly have you arriving down in the mouth.

Still, no more dwelling on the privations of the process of travelling, where to be fair you so often tend to see people at their worst. Let's be optimistic. Life is surely much better than the alternative, it may contain good times and bad, but it is largely what we make it. It was Abraham Lincoln who said that "By and large a man has the level of happiness he decides to have". It's a fair thought and one that seems to me well worth bearing in mind: a smile can both record the good times and help move us past the bad.

When this flight is over I will be in Thailand again. Set at the heart of South East Asia, this country of some 65 million people sits north of Malaysia, and to the north borders countries including Laos, Cambodia and Vietnam. It has a long history of independence, its own distinctive culture and sits in a fertile area of monsoon country; it is hot and on occasion very wet. It is known for its food, silk, elephants, temples, Buddhism and, these days, its economic growth and volatile politics. It's a major tourist destination, offering wonderful beaches, sightseeing, activities – everything from white water rafting to elephant riding – and great hospitality: the Thais love visitors to appreciate their country and many delight in helping you get to know it.

Above all, remember, this country is designated as a whole land of smiles; it also has a decidedly laid back attitude to life. One of the few Thai phrases I feel I can use accurately (and even pronounce clearly) in *mai pen rai*. If you look up this phrase in a dictionary it will say that it means something like "never mind". This is rather like saying that the temperature in Thailand is "rather warm" or that six large scotches constitutes a "little drink" and brings a whole new meaning to the concept of understatement. The word means something more like: Never mind – that's life – don't worry – it will all be the same in a hundred years – don't let's waste time or effort dwelling on it – no sweat: other things are more important – so what's next? It can be used to put over all or any part of such a sentiment and is a much used and most useful phrase, with no direct counterpart in English with anything like the same breadth of meaning. The phrase is characteristic of the happy-go-lucky attitude that seems to be so much a part of Thai life.

The phrase also acts as a way of putting things behind you. Stand in a hotel trying to check in when the computer system says you have no reservation and you will likely have a frustrating time. Do they have a room? Yes. So why not just check you in and sort anything else out later before your jetlag has you crashing and burning? But seemingly endless minutes later, you can mutter *Mai pen rai* as you step into a nice room and the trip begins to bode well again; here it means "Forget it and move on". One hotel where I have never had such things happen is Bangkok's Tawana Hotel. An independent hotel, good yet reasonably priced, in the Silom Road area, it was the first hotel I ever stayed in in Bangkok. Now they greet me like an old friend. Next they ask for my credit card to guarantee payment. "Don't you trust me?" I say. "Sure, no problem" they respond. "You have all my details on file" I add helpfully. "Yes, just sign card, not need to fill in," the receptionist says helpfully. "I've stayed here for 25 years," I add, knowing she was there the first time. "Of course, long time, no problem". She passes me the card... and adds "And your credit card, please... for the system". We both smile, she swipes the card and I enjoy the whole process.

All this seems to indicate that Thailand is a good place to avoid gloom and investigate smiles. But perhaps even the famed Thai smile can mislead. Is there more to the land of smiles than, well, smiles? I have always found that visits to Thailand act as an antidote to the kind mirthless atmosphere that seems to pervade so much of modern life; it is a country where smiling is integral to the culture and it is also a country where so many things seem to put a smile on your face. And at the start of this trip I have fixed an appointment with the Royal Institute of Thailand, a body that acts as the official keeper of the Thai smile; well actually it is the keeper of the Thai language and thus the way in which the Thai smile is described. As we come into land I wonder what that means and how the face that greets me there will look.

Prelude

Chapter One

REQUEST CONSIDERED: AUDIENCE GRANTED

"When I use a word, it means just what I choose it to mean, neither more nor less."
Lewis Carrol (said by Humpty Dumpty)

The Royal Institute of Thailand was set up in 1933, though there is a long history of earlier bodies with broadly the same brief. It is effectively a government department and describes its role as being the principal institution of the national intellectual network committed to the advancement of knowledge. What? This sounds pretty much like what many a modern business would call – rather grandly – a mission statement, but it hardly provides a clear and definitive description of its role. But one thing was clear: its Arts Division has a clear role in preserving and promoting the use of the Thai language.

Thai is a tonal language. There are four tones and 21 different sounds used to speak it. No wonder I find it difficult to learn any amount of it. For the technically minded it is one of the Tai-Kadai family of languages. It has a long history and is believed to have originated in Southern China. I quickly discovered that The Royal Institute is not in any sense a public place. I had emailed a couple of local friends about it only to be told that it was not open to the public; was there a hint there of especially not to the likes of you?

Chapter One

Nevertheless, I had then written a polite letter asking to call and talk to someone. They emailed me back promptly, but wanted to know something more about me and, after I wrote again, they still made no commitment but promised "to give my request every consideration".

I waited patiently, imagining a special meeting of government officials being called to decide if I was worthy of an audience. I wonder what they said. "Is this person legitimate/real/true/authorised/credible/passable/warranted?" I'm sure they found the right word eventually. Finally, a week or so ahead of the date I had suggested for a meeting, a polite message came giving me permission to visit.

Taxis in Bangkok used to be an adventure. When I first visited the city none had a meter, a driver who spoke English, or a history of recent maintenance. They rattled and juddered through the traffic. There was no air-con either, and the temperature – and the fumes – soared and swirled around them. You prayed for them to get a move on and get the journey over with, but if they did find a gap in the traffic and achieve any real speed you became convinced that death was imminent and prayed for deliverance. Taxis were outnumbered by Tuc-Tucs, the little three wheeled contraptions ubiquitous in Thailand that are essentially a small, roofed platform fixed behind the front end of a motorbike, and so called because of the noise they make, I think. Passengers sit on a bench seat behind the driver. Open-sided, these expose you even more to the traffic fumes and were strictly for shorter distances, though local people used them extensively and still do. Even though there are now fewer of them, it is still not unusual to see a whole family spanning three generations packed onto one groaning machine, together with mountains of packages.

Any first time visitor arriving at the airport was always recommended to use hotel or airport limousines, and the public taxis at the airport were reputed to be driven by gangsters intent not on taking you to your hotel, but on robbing you, abandoning you and leaving you senseless at the roadside. I never had or heard of such a problem actually occurring, it must be said, and now, as over the years things have modernised, the taxis are much like those in any other city. Well, mostly they are. Different companies run taxis in differing liveries: most are green, green and yellow or some such combination, but here is the only place where some favour a particularly vivid hue of fluorescent pink. Perhaps colour and taxis always have an element of the bizarre: in London the traditional cabs are always called "black cabs", whatever colour they may be.

When I arrived at the airport I went through the ritual of collecting luggage and so on promptly. The immediate exception to the rule about Thai smiles seems to be the government officials who staff passport control. Rarely do they even look at you (little cameras like black ping-pong balls alongside them do that); maybe they are told to remain dour as a reminder of the serious nature of breaching your visa terms. Determined not to pay a premium for some posh car, I went to the Departures floor, stepped outside and, welcomed by the humid heat, picked up a public taxi as it dropped someone off. It appeared modern, a Toyota like so many are, and was bright pink. This avoids any queues in the Arrivals area and guarantees a happy driver as it avoids the possibility of a long queue for them too as they move to wait

Chapter One

in Arrivals. I was thus soon speeding down the expressway that connects Bangkok's airport with the city. My driver smiled a welcome and agreed a reasonable fare.

The taxi meters, though now installed, are rarely used for journeys of any length, or for short ones in the rush hour, or for tourists who might be persuaded to take a route via a "Special jewellery shop – very cheap", or just be persuaded to pay more than the meter will likely clock up. It usually transpires that such a jewellery shop is run by the driver's brother-in-law, cousin or uncle; family connections in Thailand often seem to link to business opportunities in labyrinthine networks that aim to benefit all. Making some comments that indicated I had visited many times avoided all this; my driver promised to use the toll road and then proceeded to practise his not-bad English on me as we went. After some stock questions – "Where you from? Holiday?" – he asked why I was there. I tried to explain about my smile investigation, but his English faltered and as we came off the toll highway and into Bangkok's busy traffic he lapsed into silence and I was happy to let him concentrate on his driving. Taxi drivers rarely speak very much English, though there are exceptions, and how they converse does vary: some will say virtually nothing, others more. I once had one driver who talked non-stop: "How are you – where you from – okay – I take you see Grand Palace – okay – today – tomorrow – okay – give you telephone number – you call me – okay – I drive everywhere – go to market – find you nice girl – okay – soon – go buy jewellery..." There was no pause left for answers and his comments ran on unabated punctuated only by regular "okays". At my destination he collected the fare, but made no attempt to see if any of his many suggestions had rung a bell. It was a little like listening to a tape on a loop.

There was a sign in the back of the taxi about tooth whitening. Medical tourism now evidently embraces this cosmetic treatment; indeed, in recent times you see similar signs in many places around the world so it may have become the thing of the moment. The most popular come-on was the offer of a free foot massage if you bought the treatment. I have no idea if the two things were done simultaneously, though the picture this conjures up is intriguing. But this focus on a suitably gleaming smile was, I hoped, a good omen.

My driver dropped me at my hotel, one I had stayed at in the past. The welcome here is always cheerful. "Hello Boss, welcome to your second home," said the bell boy, giving me a broad smile and grabbing my luggage as I went to check in. Everyone here smiles. The girl at reception who checked me in, the cashier who would check me out, two or three staff members as I crossed the lobby to go to my room, and the bell boy who took me up to my room. Once I was unpacked and refreshed, I began to concentrate on my mission.

Addresses and locations in a strange city can often present problems, especially when road signs are not necessarily in English, and the hectic traffic in Bangkok is always a hazard. Most Bangkok taxi drivers are pretty good these days, though, as I've said, that may not stretch to the driver's English. At worst, though, it is possible to spend an hour doing a journey that you have been told should take twenty minutes, and then find yourself dropped in what proves to be the wrong place. Of course, in a city such as Bangkok this might prove interesting, but you could even find yourself back where you started from. Any uncertainties are best avoided when you have an

Chapter One

appointment somewhere, especially somewhere with the word Royal in its title, so the morning of my visit I started at the concierge desk in my hotel.

"I wonder, can you tell me exactly where this address is located, please?" I asked, showing them the details of the Royal Institute. It was clearly not a routine destination and produced puzzled expressions. One of the two staff members manning the desk telephoned the number and had the location described to them.

"No problem," the now smiling man said, and explained that it was not far away, adding that a public taxi would be the best and least expensive way to get there. Good – the cars available at hotels are well known for their high cost, though at least their drivers usually do speak fair English and there is an excellent chance of getting directly to your destination. Even so, if he was employed to sell his particular means of transport, recommending the opposition was hardly giving his employer value for money. Nevertheless, armed with the address, and with some directions he had written in Thai, the doorman hailed a taxi for me, lent in and explained to the driver where I wanted to go, and we set off.

After just a hundred meters, the driver, who spoke a little English, slowed, squinted uncertainly at the directions and asked to see my note again: the address on this written in English. He again professed finding it to be "no problem" and we continued on. Twenty minutes later we entered a wide empty square, a cul de sac with an imposing building facing us at the end. This, I discovered later, was part of a university. He pulled up at a gated entrance on the right hand side of the square with an open area surrounded by buildings stretching beyond. A long conversation ensued with the security guards at the gate. He relayed this on to me. We were, he had been assured, in the wrong place, but they had given him directions. We would be there in a trice. Actually "trice" was not in his vocabulary, but his smile indicated it was the right word for me to infer. We set off again, going only a few hundred metres round the block and stopping at another gated entrance.

This time, security was in the form of armed soldiers. This seemed odd. But having been assured that we were in the right place, I paid the taxi and the driver sped off. Again a long conversation ensued, this time with an armed guard and, with time until my appointment fast disappearing, I struggled to make myself understood and began to wonder if I would ever get to the right spot. It quickly transpired that I was still not yet in the right place. In fact, I was at the entrance to Chitrlada Palace, an early 20th century building surrounded by extensive grounds, gardens and lakes, and the permanent residence of the King and his family when he is Bangkok. It is a home he shares with a dozen or so rare white elephants; white elephants, which even have their own monument in Northern Thailand, are regarded as especially lucky and whenever these rare animals appear they are given to the King.

What would they do now with an unscheduled, and lost, *farang* visitor? *Farang*, incidentally, is the term used in Thailand to refer to a Caucasian foreigner; it is not an insult, if it has a connotation attached to it is probably one of regret – *So sorry, we cannot all be born Thai*. Far from sending me on my way, or drawing their weapons at the sight of a lone *farang* having pulled into the palace entrance unannounced, the soldiers may not have been going to introduce me to the

Chapter One

King, but they were helpfulness personified. Perhaps it was a slow day for real threats and they were glad of the diversion – "Not a terrorist in sight, let's keep busy by sending this poor, lost *farang* in the right direction".

An officer rapidly took charge. He led me into a small office alongside the entrance courtyard. He made a phone call, and another… and another. What was said was all in Thai, of course, and a mystery to me, but he seemed gradually to be getting nearer to an answer for me and nodded and smiled to me throughout the process. He then wrote patiently and at some length, while sending one of his troop – there were a dozen or so of them – out onto the road to hail me another taxi. I saw him stepping out into the road and waving his rifle. A driver quickly stopped – well, let's be accurate, the first taxi to appear came to an immediate and dramatic halt, its brakes squealing and its tyres emitting blue smoke. As well it might: the driver probably thought he was either about to be arrested or asked to assist with a national emergency. The officer handed over his written instruction to the driver and told me, "All okay now, no problem". Then, as I struggled to thank him, one of the soldiers held the taxi door open for me. In I got and we were off again. The palace guard who had held the door for me saluted. For a moment I felt quite grand and imagined what the taxi driver, stopped in such an abrupt fashion, might be thinking – *Who is this palace-visiting farang?* I rather hoped he did assume that I was pretty grand, but he probably realised I had just been lost.

A few minutes later, I found myself stopping for a second time at the gate to which I had first been taken and sent away from after being told firmly I was in the wrong place. But this time the officer's written note did the trick, the barrier was raised and we were allowed through. Inside the gate was a large grassed area ringed with buildings. A few had notices outside, but all were written in Thai. My driver drove slowly round the circuit twice, apparently becoming no nearer to knowing exactly where I should be, until I insisted we stop at random and I went into the nearest building to ask for directions. Finally I must surely be close, I thought. Someone at reception summoned an English-speaking colleague and my asking for directions resulted in another phone call being made. My helper then walked me out of the building and round the perimeter until I was met by the lady with whom I had the appointment coming the other way. She had come out to meet me.

Smiling a welcome, *Khun* Cholthicha looked cool despite the heat, immaculate in a bright silk outfit and totally unphased by the various phone calls she had received or by my late arrival. She gave me a polite *wai*: this is a graceful gesture in which the palms are placed together as in prayer and the hands are raised in greeting and respect. Many Thais will follow it with a handshake if they are greeting a *farang*, and certainly do not expect you to understand the full nuances of such a gesture – the height at which the hands are held depends on the relative status of the two people – but it does seem to be appreciated when you return the gesture. This is indeed a much used and characteristic gesture, one only giving me pause for thought when taxi drivers pass a shrine at the roadside and execute the gesture taking both hands off the steering wheel as they do so. I guess they reckon the spirits have control for a moment or two, certainly it does not seem to worry them.

Chapter One

Greeting done, I found that her office was only a few metres away and a few minutes later I was ensconced there with a cup of tea, being assured that the fact that I was a few minutes late was of no import and that anyway the Institute was "very difficult to find".

One thing about the English language is its enormous vocabulary, now reckoned to be more than a million words, indeed several million if you include things like medical and computer terms. Other languages rarely come anywhere near this, though they may differ in other ways. For example, the way in which grammar works certainly varies; I have had books translated into German and they appear some 25 percent longer than in English, largely because of the way German speakers their sentences do arrange. Thai may have a smaller vocabulary than English, but the Royal Institute produce a master dictionary and my informant showed me a huge volume five or six inches thick. This lists *the* way in which every Thai word is spelled (in an alphabet with 44 consonants and more vowels and other combinations and sounds) and defines exactly how each should be used. Producing this volume is no easy matter and a new edition appears only about every 10 years, its contents debated and discussed at length in the interim by a plethora of academics and committees spread around the land and working to ensure that the right decisions are made. The process is actually slowing as language becomes more international, changes faster and must accommodate a whole raft of new words, many of them linked to technology.

The only other country that I can think of that has anything like this sort of official process is France. A French committee (the Academie Française) exists mainly to preserve their unique language and protect it from invaders; even so, the French use such words as "Le Weekend" and have adopted many other English words, albeit grudgingly. They also have the separate problem of deciding whether any additional nouns that are allowed into the language are to be masculine or feminine. I once heard a story told of the discussion about the adoption of the technological word "semi-conductor". Should it be *le* or *la semi-conductor?* After long debate, the exact scientific definition was quoted: "a semi-conductor is a material the resistance of which becomes less as its temperature rises". Despite the fact that this refers to electrical resistance, once the committee heard this they unanimously decided it should be prefixed by the female, *la*. They were probably all men.

Khun Cholthicha told me that the official nature of the decisions about correct language use was, as befits a Royal Institute, taken very seriously, but that "of course" there was no means of exerting compulsion on people to speak and write correctly. Nevertheless, the staff at the Institute liaised with the educational world on a regular basis and ran what was effectively a public relations campaign promoting correct use. This included a daily radio programme and the distribution of CDs to schools. I can't imagine any British institution doing a similar job. There is the Plain English Campaign, but, however worthy and worthwhile, it is a small private organisation hardly at the heart of any public debate. Certainly, the British government, far from running a campaign for good English, nowadays even allows pupils in state schools to pass exams with such things as poor spelling barely even mentioned. Maybe I should write to the Secretary of State for Education about it. Or send a text: Plz do smthng

Chapter One

2 imprv da stndrd of spkn & wrttn Eng in skools. I am sure I would be understood, but I doubt any action would result.

I admired what the Royal Institute did and the seriousness with which its staff clearly interpreted its role with regard to language. Evidently few visitors drop in to see what they are up to, and fewer still from overseas, I fancy. But my guide was unstinting in her hospitality and at pains to explain to me all that they did. They have a job these days, too. There are many languages in Thailand, with many of the hill tribes in the north having their own language. Some, like that of the *Akha* people, exist only in spoken form. The *Akha* have a story that a written language was once delivered to them by the first spirit *Un Ma*. It was, however, written on an animal skin and, before it could be assimilated, they ate it! But then food has always been important in Thailand. Today the minority languages are declining as young people learn English to enable them to use Facebook and other social media. It is classic Thai that is the Royal Institute's concern, however.

Khun Cholthicha also told me something about the matter of smiles in Thailand. The Thai word for smile is *yim*, and there are certainly a variety of different – indeed officially designated – kinds of smile. These range from *yim tang nam dtah*, which is a genuinely happy smile of pleasure, a top of the range lottery win kind of smile that is, to the *yim soo*. The second is best described as a "the situation is so bad that it cannot possibly get any better so the best thing to do is smile" smile. Beats bursting into tears, I guess. These are just two of the many variations the Institute have listed.

Others include *yim tak tai*, a polite smile directed at people you do not know well. *Yim cheuat cheuan* is a happy smile directed at someone less happy; when someone gets into the last parking space in the car park just ahead of someone else, this would be the smile directed at the less fortunate driver. *Fuen yim* is the airport smile, the "I have to smile but don't want to smile" smile. *Yim tak tan* has an apologetic feel while indicating "I'm right and you're wrong" and *yim cheun chom* is an admiring smile. *Yim sao* masks feelings of sadness or unhappiness. *Yim yair-yair* and *yim hairng* are similar, the first indicating an apology designed to reduce the heat of a situation and the second being more personal – a kind of apology and a request that anger is not directed at the person doing the smiling combined. *Yim mai ork*, literally the smile that can't be made, is an inadequate smile because, for whatever reason, it just doesn't work.

Sometimes a smile has more negative connotations: *yim yor* is a mocking smile intended to be unpleasant and *yim mee lay-nai* is a smile of evil intent, the "I am about to rip you off or do you down" smile. Confusion is always possible: spill your drink all over yourself in a bar and you will see people smile: it will not be a *yim yor*, that's a smile laughing at your misfortune, but more often a *yim yair-yair* designed to prevent you feeling embarrassed. And, of course, if another customer spills your drink there will also be a smile: hopefully a *yim yair-yair*, a smile of apology. It may be difficult to follow and interpret them all, but there is more than enough here to illustrate why the land of smiles got its nickname. The number of different smiles varies, depending on who you talk to, 10, 13, 15? And one informant told me seriously, "Whichever number is correct there are 10 versions of each of them."

There are many variations, not because of the Institute – its deliberations simply reflect how the language is – but rather because the smile really is an important element of the way Thai culture and communication works. I took my leave, receiving another graceful *wai* from my informant, resolving to investigate further. The taxi that took me back to my hotel delivered an uneventful ride, there were no diversions to any more palaces, no further interventions by armed soldiers and even the level of traffic was low enough for me to permit myself a slight smile.

Back at the hotel I counted six smiles of greeting from staff as I made my way back to my room.

Chapter Two

THE ELEPHANTS' SMILE

Nature's great masterpiece, an elephant,
The only harmless great thing.
John Donne

After investigating smiles through official channels it was, at first, a little difficult to know where to add to that view. Elephants are familiar from a thousand television wildlife programmes, zoo visits and, on some occasions, as the pink creatures of our hangovers. But in Thailand, elephants are a living national symbol and many statues and as a result images are created to represent them. A well-known Thai artist, Anurak Chaijit, has carved more than a hundred elephants from teak. One of his pieces is called "Elephant's sweet smile" and evidently depicts an elephant laughing. Other artworks are said to feature smiling elephants and a real live Thai elephant has garnered some fame as a painter. Noppakhao, as he is called, wields brushes with what his proud owner calls "jumbo talent" and produces pictures – including some of elephants – good enough to pass for paintings by human hand and indeed good enough to sell on the open market. I bet he really does smile; even if he doesn't, his owner is doubtless laughing all the way to the bank. There is probably some artistic license at work with all of this, but given the importance of elephants in Thailand, I wondered if there might be a germ of truth in it too – maybe elephants do smile.

Thus, elephants had to be part of my investigation of smiles.

In Thailand, elephants are not only important, they are also regarded as bringing good luck. To be truly lucky an elephant image has to have its trunk raised – a stance that is actually symbolic of overcoming obstacles – and many statues and images are represented this way as a result. What happens in real life I am not sure; maybe elephant keepers spend half their time running round holding a banana up high on a stick so that their elephants raise their trunks to reach for it and thus bring them good luck. So important are elephants that, until quite recently, the Thai flag bore a white elephant on a bright red background. I had not actually seen one of the special white elephants kept at the Chitrlada Palace during my brief stop there, though I knew they were there.

A mere handful of elephants are rare white ones. I don't know why I am measuring elephants in handfuls; elephants are more usually used to describe the weight of other things: a London bus weighs the same as two elephants, for instance. But I digress. A white elephant is a rare beast and is regarded as too noble an animal to undertake anything mundane, only Royal duties are deemed appropriate; indeed, such an animal is regarded as existing to enhance the King's honour and glory in a way that is believed to promote prosperity and happiness around the kingdom. This makes them sound important and special, which indeed they are, but it was these same creatures that gave rise to the expression "a white elephant" being used to describe something useless. Strictly, a white elephant in this sense refers to something for which the cost, especially of upkeep, exceeds the usefulness of it. The Thai Royal white elephants may have inspired the phrase and may incur high upkeep costs, but they are not thought of as useless – far from it. Promoting happiness and prosperity is surely not just useful but important; anyway, all that apart it's a nice tradition.

Amongst some 5000 elephants that live in Thailand, nearly half of them domesticated and working, either to entertain tourists or help harvest timber, only a handful are white ones. Anyone discovering a white elephant must, by law, report it to the Ministry of the Interior. Perhaps it's a bit like the cone hotlines on Britain's motorways, and there are signs in rural areas with a special "elephant number" to call. Report it I am sure people do, first because such traditions are enjoyed and respected here and secondly because, well you can't very easily hide any sort of elephant so honesty is probably the best policy.

The ministry, in turn, must notify the Royal household of such a find and this triggers a process of official verification. Any potential white elephant must undergo a physical examination to make sure it is truly a white one. This is something consisting of much more than a cursory glance: it involves an examination of many parts of the elephant – its skin, hair, tail, eyes and tonsils – even its more intimate parts. Given that a successful examination means that an elephant will qualify for a life of comfort at the Royal palace, they may be quite sanguine about all this being done. But perhaps white elephant verification is a somewhat hazardous job and elephants do not take kindly to certain elements of it. Several tons of elephant, white or otherwise, taking exception to having its private bits poked at cannot be a walk in the park for the investigator. I am not sure how this examination is done, or who does it. Does the Royal household have a "White Elephant Verification Officer" and, if so, is this a full time job? Perhaps they double as a butler or have other duties to keep them busy between discoveries. Or do they call someone in from outside?

Anyway, once verified as a *Chang Samkhan*, as a white elephant is called, the King is informed and a ceremony takes place to officially recognise it as a Royal white elephant, one that will in future be honoured rather as a prince. This whole process, something which has gone on for at least 500 years, is an important tradition. The process is regarded as displaying gratitude to elephants out of respect for their role in Thai culture. In years past, this role has included an important military aspect and elephants once carried people into battle. As a result of all this, Thailand's current King, like many of his predecessors, numbers amongst his many titles that of "King of the white elephants".

Interesting though white elephants may be, they are only few in number, and though distinctly different to regular elephants, they are in any case not strictly white but more a pinkish grey colour. I have seen regular elephants perform at tourist sites in the past, something that they appeared to do with extreme patience and considerable grace. Though certainly there were moments in the performance when the handler – the *mahout* – could easily be injured if an elephant took a serious dislike to the proceedings. Having seen this, I decided that any investigation would be better done with wild elephants. Because of the considerable efforts made nationally to protect and encourage elephants in Thailand, there are numbers of habitats set aside for them.

So it was that I found myself on a woodland path in a country area outside Hua Hin, a town a couple of hours south of Bangkok set on the coast and where the King has his summer palace. A loud crashing in the scrub alongside the path indicated the unmistakable presence of elephants. These elephants hadn't a care in the world and were just busy doing what elephants do, in this case rampaging across the track to join their fellows on the other side and woe betide anyone who might get in their way.

As I have said, elephants are regularly seen in Thailand. On more than one occasion I have seen them holding up traffic as they amble slowly along a Bangkok street. After all it's not all temples, markets and beaches in this popular holiday destination; many visitors see elephants, trained to perform, at places like the Rose Garden close to Bangkok, where they are part of a show that includes graceful Thai dancing. There are also a considerable number of working elephants gainfully employed and hauling logs to supply the world with teak wood. These undergo lengthy training, are highly prized and usually well looked after, but they must lead a busy life – all pull, pull, pull or push, push, push. Given the stresses of work, what would the average working elephant want to do on its day off? Where do elephants dream of going on holiday?

Well, less than an hour away from Hua Hin is Kuiburi National Park. Here a huge 600 square miles of beautiful countryside is set aside solely for elephants. Bar a few tracks and simple buildings used by the wardens, there is nothing here but the open country: woods, grasslands, hills and lakes.

Chapter Two

Farmers nearby used to resent the animals, which regularly damaged their crops. Understandably, producing pristine pineapples is somewhat difficult if they are regularly crushed under the big flat feet of several tons of elephant. A solution was found. Now the farmers are paid to plant elephant treats within the reserve, keeping the elephants away from the farms and giving extra income to the rural farmers too. Now everyone's happy.

Driving out from Hua Hin, one quickly leaves the town behind, then any sign of habitation becomes rare. Turning off the road, the car arranged to take me to the area entered the reserve and made its way around a huge lake. Before going further we were invited to go out on the lake in a boat. Some fishermen had been alerted to our arrival and came towards the shore. Their boats were tiny. I could practically have floated one in my bath. Nevertheless, they insisted we had a ride and some of us skimmed along sitting in front of the helmsman as he worked a tiny outboard motor. The view was lovely, but with the extra weight of a passenger the water lapped a little into the boat as I went. It was little more than a dugout canoe and hardly ideal for its owner plus a large *farang*. I hope these fishermen make a good living, but it seemed to me that a really good catch would sink the boat.

The countryside around was completely unspoiled, the lake shone in the sun below a cloudless sky and, through 360 degrees, were just rolling hills with no sign of any human habitation. Once ashore again, we got back in the car. In due course, the car drew up alongside an isolated colonial style wooden building with a covered terrace along the front that made me expect Clint Eastwood to step out any moment to toss his cheroot away.

Ask a Thai what their national sport is and, while they may mention their passion for Manchester United or some other football club, they will more likely tell you that they rank eating above even that. Or they will if they don't have their mouths full, and can actually speak. So naturally the first thing to do on arrival was have lunch. Boating, well boating like that, gives you an appetite. A delicious spread consisting of fish, chicken, vegetables and rice was laid out on a covered terrace. It took the best part of an hour to get through; the pineapple that followed was so perfect that botanists might well have catalogued it as a separate species from the so often tired equivalent which we see imported into Europe. A cold beer added to the meal's excellence and conversation flowed around the table amongst the handful of visitors other than ourselves as the midday sun beat down a few metres away.

Now replete, the next thing to do was to spend three-quarters of an hour in an aged pick-up truck bouncing along rough tracks deep into elephant country. Few tourists come here; no other single soul was visible all day. This visit had been arranged by a local friend and someone I later recommended visit there, returned from Hua Hin saying that they could find no one in the town able to arrange it. The roads and vehicle were anything but modern and the ride was more than a little bumpy. The countryside was awe-inspiring and we rested and drank tea at another small building, sitting looking down into a small ravine through which ran a bubbling river. The building was little more than a shack, but visitors could stay here overnight and it must surely have been a wonderful spot first thing in the morning. Water and bird song apart, the silence was palpable, the setting idyllic.

Chapter Two

The elephants were clearly lucky to live in a nation prepared to give up this amount of prime countryside to conserve and encourage them, and protect them from the dangers of the modern world.

As we drove on, the guide stopped the truck and suggested walking a little way along the track. All he said was, "Quietly". First they could be heard. Either side of the track was woodland, not the sort of country even a small elephant could move through without making a noise. Then a group – a family perhaps – were visible amongst the trees to the right.

"By that tree, by that tree," whispered our guide, pointing to a spot maybe 50 metres away. There seemed to be six or seven elephants, large and small, but the small sapling indicated was abruptly uprooted, upended and the green top devoured by one of the larger ones. Then more elephants were audible, and then visible, on the other side of the path, both groups now perhaps only 20 or 30 metres off. Suddenly the guide looked worried. "Dangerous, dangerous," he said and led the way quickly back to the truck.

As one group of elephants crossed the path to join the others at a brisk pace, their feet thudded on the dry earth and reddish dust rose into the air. I am not sure that they were aware of us watching; if they were, I am sure we rated only a momentary thought – *A few visitors in this evening, Dad. Just ignore them, or you might encourage them, Son.* In any case, they looked neither to left or right and one would not have wanted to be in their way. This was their place and they clearly felt able to go exactly where they wanted, and did just that. Some care was clearly necessary for anyone spending time on their territory. The guide was passionate about his work. "Good job, good job," he said. "Must take care.

Elephant very important, very beautiful." He was right; I am sure it is an important job and one that must be satisfying to do as well.

Later, sitting on a high ridge looking across a valley, I watched the sun set slowly behind the trees and elephants moved – graceful and serenely – across the grassland way below, through the cool of the evening. They were too far away to see if they were smiling or not, but apparently unconcerned by spectators, they looked as if they knew they were safe. Content in these natural surroundings and with their lot, they disappeared into the evening gloom. Smiling or not, they seemed happy. Their environment may be managed to a degree, but these were truly wild elephants. Quizzing them further about their ability to smile just wasn't possible, though the guide assured me that they did: "Oh yes, I know, I see," he said firmly. This was a special place to visit; I felt privileged to have done so at a time when few tourists apparently knew of it, and I left concluding that any working elephant could do much worse than book their holidays in such a spot.

Elephants are obviously large creatures. For instance, they drink some 60 gallons of water each day and eat 600lbs of food. If they need care, and some do, especially those rescued from difficult circumstances or neglect or abuse, it is an expensive business. There are various schemes and charities in Thailand that help and you can indeed adopt an elephant (check out *www.adoptelephants.org*).

Naturalists declare that elephants are well known to express emotion. They appear to grieve, and seeing two old elephant friends meeting is to observe a whole range of emotions, including, it is said, love and joy. If elephants really

Chapter Two

can smile, and certainly their features can present what looks very like one, then those elephants resident in this impressive reserve probably smile an "aren't I lucky to be here, my home cosseted by wardens, an ideal environment and pretty much not a care in the world" sort of smile. *Yim* followed by a few other words, no doubt.

Given their undoubted good fortune, the very least that they can do is to raise their trunks occasionally to bring some good luck to the rest of us.

Chapter Three

WHAT'S IN STORE?

Today you're unhappy? Can't figure it out?
What is the salvation? Go shopping.

Arthur Miller

The modern capital of Thailand, Bangkok, is a huge sprawling city that is home to more than ten million people. It also has the longest place name in the world: in full it is *Krung threp mahanakhon bovorn ratanakosin mahintharayutthaya mahadilok pop noparatratchathani burirom udomratchanietmahasathan amornpiman avatarnsathit sakkathattiyavisnukarmprasit* – to save you counting, that's 167 letters. No wonder they abbreviate it to *Krung Thep* – City of Angels. I bet envelope manufacturers went into recession when they did that and large sized envelopes were no longer necessary to accommodate the name in addresses.

It is a hectic place. The traffic is notorious and it has something of the concrete jungle about it. It is a city I find numbers of first time visitors fail to be enamoured by, but when that happens I suspect they have picked a poorly located hotel and struggle to get about and see anything worthwhile, probably on a short visit. Long journeys across the city, and long times spent in traffic jams, do not give a good impression. In recent years the sky train, a train running above the traffic, and an increasing number of express highways, though these can have their moments, have helped. It is a place that takes a while to get the measure of, but, despite the pollution and the traffic, doing so is well worthwhile. Both some of its major sights, and its less known corners, are a delight, as is its overall atmosphere. So too is the river bisecting it, the Chao Phraya, which is a busy, working river, fast and wide and which runs on a further 10 miles or so to the sea.

Stay near the river, is my advice, though overall there is enormous choice from backpacker guest houses to main chain hotels, and everything in between. There is even one small hotel, The Ibrik, right on the river and so small it has only three rooms. It is fun to wake up and step out onto a wooden balcony only a few feet above the water of the river with the many boats that use the waterway, from tiny one-person personal transports to river buses that travel the length and breadth of the waterfront, passing by. Also in evidence are the "trains" of barges, sometimes as many as 10 tethered in line, laden down to the gunnels and pulled by motor launches that seem several sizes too small for the job. These all have small "houses" on top of one of the barges and for whole families that is home. A huge network of *klongs* (canals) run off the main channel of the river. These have reduced in number over the years. Bangkok was once called the Venice of the East, but those that remain are still very characteristic of the place: they are effectively streets and have homes, shops and more along their length.

The main sites are well known. The best known is probably the Grand Palace, a huge area that is also home to *Phra Kaeo*, the Emerald Buddha. Take care going there for the first time as touts will always tell you it is closed for a while, offering to take you on a short trip and returning when it reopens. Do that, and for the most part you will waste a couple of hours being offered everything from silks to jewellery in shops that always seem to be run by a relative of your driver. Thais love tourists, they respect how important they are to the national economy and they genuinely like to meet people and tell them about their country, after all they also sympathise – for no fault of your own you have not been born Thai. But many also take the view that everyone can be conned, albeit in a small way for the most part, at least once. All such relationships change when you make clear you have been to Bangkok before and or know something of the place and how things work.

There are, of course, temples everywhere, their beautifully shaped roofs odd looking amongst modern buildings, their gold decoration reflecting the sun. *Wat Phra Chetuphon* – known as Wat Pho – is the largest and oldest. This dates back to the 16th century and houses the famous reclining Buddha, which is some 150 feet long. It is a busy area with a variety of activities being carried on there, for instance a traditional medicine centre. Like the Grand Palace, the best known temple, *Wat \Arun*, is on the river. Tall and covered with thousands of pieces of porcelain that sparkle in the sunlight, this is a magnet for tourists; you can climb right to the top and get a great view along the river. It is also the place to go to see massed groups of Japanese busy photographing each other. But it is at its best when it is quiet so those visiting early in the morning do well. There is a monastery behind it and few people venture through that area, but it is not only beautiful, all old style Thai buildings, but there are often robed monks around, some of whom are happy to talk and tell you about the place and their lives.

Chapter Three

This is not a guidebook, however, and I have no intention of providing a comprehensive run down in that form. Let me focus, though, on one aspect of Thailand that is certainly ubiquitous: that of markets. Britain was once called a nation of shopkeepers, meaning, before Starbucks and chain stores took over the world, that there were many small, independent retail businesses. Despite the best efforts of Tesco, whose big shops run in a local partnership as Tesco Lotus and do very well, it is similar in Thailand, but the greatest number is in the form of market stalls. These themselves vary across a wide range, from stalls in huge markets to just a handful gathered together in some small corner, and even those that are mobile: there seem to be small, cycle-based stalls on every corner, especially selling food. Indeed, I have heard it said that it is a country where care is necessary in case you are run over by a shop. Such an accident must sometimes occur and it must be interesting if the police are involved. They cannot ask if the victim got the registration number, and answering the "Would you recognise it again?" question would doubtless be followed by something akin to a restaurant critique – "Well, the spring rolls were unexceptional, but the flavour of the beef soup – I've got it all down my shirt – was wonderful. I'd recognise that anywhere."

Bangkok is famous for its markets and a visit to one of the big ones is a must for any visitor. The best known, often just referred to as *the* "Weekend Market" is Chatuchak. Certainly the largest such place in the country, it is a massive conglomeration of some 6,000 stalls, a veritable city in market form. Other markets exist around the city, either on their own or, commonly now, incorporated into other areas of shops and restaurants. Some markets sell only one thing –

food, for instance or just fish. Others are more general and Chatuchak sells absolutely everything from tea towels to live snakes. The stallholders are entrepreneurs par excellence. I once saw and overheard a man negotiating a price for a kitchen knife. The stallholder pressed on, talking of the wonderful meal to come and how it would be inadequate without a full set of cutlery. That sold, he added some plates, then a complete dinner service, a dining table and six chairs. As his customer left I asked him about his salesmanship, and how he had sold so much when all that was wanted was a knife. "No, not knife," said the stallholder "He come for aspirin for his wife." I expressed amazement. "I tell him big headache mean no sex this weekend, might as well have big dinner." I exaggerate, but you do need your wits about you and it is easy to be carried away. You see tourists there, of course, but this is essentially for locals and a visit there is not just to shop, it is a fun and social occasion.

Whatever the market may be, large or small, everyone with a stall seems to have a tale to tell and even a few visits, or better still purchases, sees you invited to become privy to the affairs of the stall holder. One small purchase that is always made on my visits to Thailand is lemongrass. The plant is ubiquitous in Thailand, though it originated in India, and is literally a grass, tall, perennial and known by a variety of names such as camel grass, barbed wire grass and oil grass. Its formal name is *Cymbopogon* and there are more than 50 different species. It is much used in cooking in Thailand, being added to everything from curry to fish and poultry dishes. It is also used to make a refreshing tea.

From the citronella oil extracted from it come other useful products: soap, believed to be antifungal and have antiseptic

Chapter Three

properties, candles and mosquito repellent. Its pesticide properties and other qualities mean it is also used in the preservation of ancient manuscripts, softening the material and preventing humidity that can otherwise render texts invisible. The oil is also burnt for its fragrant smell and you can come across this in many places varying from restaurants to public toilets. It is a versatile and useful plant, surely the veritable Swiss army knife of grasses, yet one used much more sparingly in the west. If the grass cuttings from my garden had even a fraction of its usefulness I would be rich.

One tiny stall in a small arcade of shops and stalls is the place to replenish the supplies of soap and oil to take home. Why here? It is first choice because the owner, a Thai lady who speaks good English, is so welcoming. On a first visit she will take time to offer advice, allowing customers to smell the soaps and try samples of the many oils she sells. Once you are a regular, if you express an interest she will chat. Over a number of visits she described a little about herself, not least that she had a *farang* boyfriend, an American, and that the young man who helped her man the stall was her brother. On one visit only the brother was there; she was in the States and a baby was due. On the next visit she was back, a tiny baby in a crib alongside the stall ready to be shown to and admired by all. The boyfriend was back in the States and, although she has not gone to live there – "many family here to take care", good relations seem to exist and to begin with she visited him regularly with the baby. More recently, though support continues, this seems to have declined. It is, I suspect, a not uncommon story.

Now the baby is growing bigger, running about amongst the stalls. I guess it will not be long before he is running the stall as well as rings round his mother, uncle and their customers. Already he has a beautiful smile, one that shines doubly bright when he perceives someone of whom his mother approves. All this makes a simple purchase a real pleasure. If you want to find her go to the Marriott hotel (actually now called the Anantara) on the river and the stall is amongst others in the small shop and restaurant complex behind the hotel.

*

While mentioning markets, another area deserves comment: a couple of hundred yards of minor city street, close to the Silom business area, it is quiet with minimal traffic and people and, during the day, appears wholly ordinary. There is a convent nearby, a variety of shops and bars along its length, and the ubiquitous McDonalds at both ends. At around five in the afternoon a transformation takes place. Gradually, people appear, in ones and twos to start with, they begin to form groups along the length of the road. The comparative silence is submerged in a rising chatter. People now hold sway and any traffic winds its way amongst them, conceding that right of way is no longer theirs, and favouring only whichever side of the road allows them to make progress.

Now, as if on an unspoken signal, people start work. The ends of the street are blocked and a daily ritual proceeds at a steady pace, though it would be fascinating to replay on a time-lapse film, which would show the street transformed in what appeared to be a matter of minutes. Hidey holes are opened up at the side of the road: gaps between buildings turn out to be storage areas, their cavernous recesses stretching back from the street into dark, mysterious tunnels.

The first thing to emerge is a tangled mass of metal poles; these are clipped together rather like a primitive child's construction kit, long practice allowing people to identify which pieces from the plethora of lengths go where. The clattering noise of metal on metal joins the chatter and shouted instructions are added as people work together in twos and threes and small groups; suddenly the thoroughfare is end-to-end activity and noise as the metal structures fill and block the whole street.

Quickly it becomes clear that what is being assembled are the shells of market stalls; wooden boards are now brought out and placed to form the surface of the stalls, canvass is secured to create makeshift covers above. This will be necessary if – or rather when – tropical rains come, and the canvass covers some of the aisles between the stalls as well as providing protection for the goods to be sold. Finally, to escalating noise, large metal trunks are dragged out from the side of the road. Padlocks are removed. These contain the stallholders' wares: designer clothes, watches like Rolex and Longines, CDs and cassettes, all of doubtful origin, ornaments, jewellery and more. Stallholders often refer to items as "genuine fakes", and where jewellery is in the form of Buddha image or other pendants they are always guaranteed to bring good luck – "Yes, sure, all tested well". The range of luck can be very specific: you can buy an amulet to protect you during travel or even something ensuring you have a boy baby, which is likely to prove correct 50 percent of the time, after all!

Despite the heat and the apparent chaos, the work is completed without hitch and by six o'clock, as the brief twilight quickly turns to darkness, everything is ready for business. Already there are customers winding their way along the lines of stalls as the metal trunks disappear below the display areas. Lights flicker above the goods displayed for sale and a tangle of twisted electric wires hang everywhere in ad hoc chaos and then run along the surface of the road, disappearing into the storage areas where they presumably tap into the power. It looks, and I suspect is, an arrangement that would give any European Health and Safety inspector sleepless nights. Here, the danger of toasting a few tourists is evidently regarded as a normal commercial risk.

The Pat Pong Road night market is underway. From now until early in the morning, the atmosphere will be one of noisy trade, music playing from pirate CDs, stallholders shouting and customers struggling through the packed stalls, jostling each other, marvelling at the sights and bartering to get a bargain. No quarter is given and many first-time visitors will pay over the odds until they work out what the going rate really is, and how to get it.

The name Pat Pong, in fact a complex of three streets running parallel to each other, is also synonymous with Bangkok's somewhat notorious night life; it is also a red light district. This is something local publishers seem to find a good market in cataloguing with aptly titled books such as *No money, no honey*. Even so, it is perhaps worth just a few words here. Years ago, before the night market took root here, the street was lined with bars and this aspect of its nature was perhaps much more obvious. Now, to an extent, the market disguises such activity and most people visiting the market

Chapter Three

are probably there to shop, eat and drink. But the bars are certainly still there. Some are go-go bars: you can glimpse scantily clad dancers gyrating on stages and counters inside as absurdly loud music washes out of the open doors and floods the street. Whatever may prompt people go into these establishments, it is certainly not conversation. Others have live music, at least later in the evening, and still others are really just pub-like. In the latter it is possible to go in and have a drink and not notice that the girl who serves you will also accompany you home if you wish. Some of the girls are pushier than others, and all will hustle people to buy them a drink as they receive a small payment for every glass sold.

There is a bright garishness about all this. Touts offer massage all along the street (the touts, not the massage): "You want massage," they say. "You want sexy young lady." Such blandishments are always said without the sound of a question mark at the end and, if you say no, the alternatives are there in an instant: "Okay, have two young girls", "Have young man." Thailand is famous for its massage, and of course many of them are simply designed to relax you or even have genuine beneficial effects. Because it is inexpensive, well in most places, Thais will go for a massage just as you might go for a drink to relax after work. Tourists are encouraged, certainly in hot spots like Pat Pong, towards the sort of massage that, let us say, focusses more on some parts of the body than others.

Incidentally, a "no" said in Thai – sounding like "*My Ow*" – is more likely to get any sort of tout to desist than one in English. Adding the sound *krup* if you are a man – *Mai ow krup* – or *ka*, if you are a woman, makes it less abrupt; this is in fact the case with many phrases. Signs flicker outside bars advertising both drinks, prices, happy hour deals and in some case the girls; sometimes this is done in jocular terms – "20 lovely ladies and a few ugly ones". Some bars are upstairs and a rip-off is more likely in those. This is especially so if they offer *Live Shows*, a description that, in the "menus" proffered by their persistent touts, makes mere striptease appear tame; careful as you go in, you may be hit in the eye by a fast moving table tennis ball. So I'm told – I shall say no more.

Unsavoury? Salacious? Exploitative? Or all three? You decide. Though I did once see an elderly European couple emerge down a flight of stairs onto the street from such a place with the woman saying, "Well! I wish I'd seen *that* years ago." People sometimes find that there is a high cover charge in such a place, one that is not advertised in advance and which it is difficult to avoid when you have spent some time there and had a few beers. For those of a different persuasion, Pat Pong 3 houses similar activities for the gay community. Despite some of what goes on, it does not really appear sordid; certainly the Thais have a relaxed attitude to it all and a local would never think of not going to a cosy bar just because some of the hostesses were, let us say, doing more than acting as waitresses.

That the red light side of Pat Pong is taken for granted locally and regarded as unremarkable is confirmed by a news item that I remember seeing in the *Bangkok Post*, the city's main English language newspaper. It reported that two young ladies hired by an elderly German tourist and who presumably had proved too energetic for him had reported him dead in his hotel room; not an everyday occurrence, one hopes. The story, though, was not about the tourist, who for all I know was sitting on a cloud saying, "What a way to go!"

but about how, despite his death, the young ladies were taking steps to get paid because, as one of them was quoted as saying, "Business done before dead".

While I am sure that there are also other illegalities around, and certainly there is some drunkenness (amongst tourists) late in the evening, the infamous regime of Bangkok's prisons keeps drug dealing and the like pretty well controlled, or at least largely invisible. All that said, there is very little street crime in Bangkok. I certainly feel safer walking through the market here than in many parts of London these days.

Where there is somewhere to sit outside the market is a perfect people-watching place, though it's hot, of course, and that often prompts the sale of cold beer. *Singha* is the main local brew, a strong lager beer with a distinctive taste that seems to go well with Thai food and the heat. There are other brands and, certainly in Bangkok, it is now popular to drink foreign beers, Heineken being the most widely available. When in Rome though – *Singha* is good and costs less than the imports. Few Thais shop in the market here, but tourists and others come in all shapes and sizes, some returning to a stall, regularly used, to buy another movie or whatever; others exploring tentatively and with care or some trepidation. Sometimes, later in the evening, there can be some aggression as people leave the bars round about, perhaps the worse for drink, and try to make an impossible deal. On other occasions there are interactions that could only occur here.

For instance, on one occasion I observed real upset. The couple were not just upset and the man, a fit looking fellow in his 30s, apparently had a black belt in tongue-fu and violent back up was seemingly not far behind. His attractive wife had a look that combined upset and an air of here-we-go-again that suggested her partner was inclined to be volatile. It appeared he had a short fuse. But maybe in this case it could be excused: the stallholder, backed up against the display of shirts he had been attempting to sell, had evidently accused the man of being married to a lady-boy. Transvestites are certainly in evidence in Thailand: you sometimes see groups of them on the streets and many make a living as entertainers. Not just on the fringes, either; I have seen more than one New Year extravaganza where such an act has featured and there are complete shows offered to tourists all over Bangkok and beyond.

But here, the lady in question seemed unequivocally female and the man, brandishing raised fists, shouted in protest, "That's no lady-boy that's my wife, you…" His tirade of profanities intensified as the stand-off continued. The Thai man, not much more than a youth dressed in a T-shirt and jeans, protested his innocence in poor English. "No, no, no," he kept saying, "Lady-boy, lady-boy." The man became conscious of people around him staring, frankly awaiting developments, and calmed slightly or at least quietened for a moment. The lull allowed the Thai's poor pronunciation to be made out as he continued to protest. He was not saying, and had not said, "Lady-boy", but "Lady buy" – not an ill-judged insult, rather no more than an attempt to rustle up business. The man finally took the point, looked a bit sheepish, muttered under his breath and everyone drifted away. Pushing T-shirts can clearly be a dangerous business, but would surely be made easier by a minimum ability to communicate in English if your target audience is tourists.

Chapter Three

Unabashed the stallholder fixed on his next target customer and continued, "T-shirt, very cheap, happy hour: buy one get one free. Lady-boy, lady-boy."

Amid so many similar stalls, and the many selling apparently identical items, one is different from the rest. At a small, square card table under what looks like a large garden umbrella, a man incongruously wearing a top hat sells magic tricks. Dice that disappear, rings that are apparently less solid than they look, packs of cards subtly changed from regular packs. His technique is simple. He demonstrates, playing the part of magician and putting on an impromptu show, and he is very good at it too. There is manifestly nothing up his sleeve: his t-shirt has none. He collects quite a crowd, and the deal is simple: if you buy a trick then you get a private demonstration of how it works. As I watch, he whirls an apparently empty wooden cylinder round his head, bangs it down on the table, then upends it to reveal a glass vase containing water and some stunning red roses. A red rose goes to each purchaser, so he will get through a few in an evening. It seems that whoever sells roses along this road is not missing a trick either. The magician is clever, beguiling and irresistible – magic, just like the market.

*

Another area where market stalls are an essential element, and one manifestly not there primarily to cater for tourists, is Chinatown, a hotchpotch of market, homes, offices and shrines. "Vibrant" hardly covers it; it is many people's classic idea of what the "exotic east" is like and a visit here is bound to make you smile.

Ratchawong pier is just one of many on the river, its steel landing floating up and down on the tides and wobbling as the wash of passing boats gives it a nudge. It's a pretty undistinguished landing and when one of the express boats sets you down there, whistles blasting out as the crew communicate with the helmsman along its length, nothing is immediately apparent to single it out. Beyond it, though, lies Bangkok's bustling Chinatown. This is one of the oldest parts of Bangkok, set up by Chinese traders in the early 1700s. Once clear of the landing area, a busy road appears and the Chinese style of buildings and decorations are immediately apparent. Yaowarat Road is the main thoroughfare through the district; it is a road that twists and turns in a way that is said to resemble a dragon's curvy body, something that Chinese traders thought auspicious for business success. Probably they still do, after all not all dragons breathe fire and eat virgins. My youngest granddaughter tells me very seriously that those that appear in her storybooks are all "friendly dragons".

The shops and stalls here all have a Chinese feel, their decoration is for the most part red and gold and the people are also somewhat different in appearance to the native Thais. There are banners aplenty fluttering in the wind. Every major city seems to have its Chinatown and many share a common look. Here, the few main streets inland of the pier may be unmistakably Chinese, but it is in the alleyways that connect the streets and criss-cross amongst them that the character of the place is most pronounced. On one visit, I turned right at random into what proved to be a typical alley. It was maybe only two, perhaps two and a half,

Chapter Three

paces wide and busy with people moving each way and lingering by the shops that lined each side.

On my last visit I saw very few *farang*, only four in a couple of hours of wandering, and, curiously for Thailand, I was not constantly accosted by shop owners. Somehow, despite the number of people, many two-wheeled luggage trolleys loaded with stock managed to find a path through the throng. So too did a number of motor bikes patiently picking their way through and patiently tolerated as they made slow progress. Their petrol fumes added to, and for a moment overpowered, the prevailing smells of food and spices as their various loads tottered behind the riders. I noticed that, in recognition of this, a few people wore white surgical masks over their mouths and noses.

There seemed to be hundreds of little wheeled cooking shops also threading their way through the crowds and doing good business too, selling their wares as the smoke from their burners wafted about, taking time to clear the narrow alley and the awnings projecting from many shops. The food was varied. Some was recognisable: spring rolls, fish, squid and then – who knows – one stall seemed to be selling the weird fried alien spawn from a B movie. I asked what they were, but the cook spoke no English; she smacked her lips in a gesture that seemed to indicate they were delicious. "*A-roi?*" I asked and she grinned and nodded vigorously in confirmation. I took her word for it; they were just too scary looking to try.

The shops and stalls went on and on: cheap clothes and what looked like enough shoes to kit out the whole of China, never mind Thailand; buttons, beads, costume jewellery; dolls and other toys; fabric, ribbon and much more. Others were specifically Chinese: herbal medicine, spices, and religious paraphernalia. Some shops had notices saying "Wholesale only" and one sold nothing but small garish plastic representations of cakes. When I looked puzzled about these, the shop's owner shrugged and smiled, a look that seemed to say "Yes, awful, but if I can make money selling them, then I should worry". The one indication of something really different to all this was several gold shops, replete with gold rings and chains, the kind of things Chinese people the world over love to buy to store some of their wealth in a physical, status-enhancing asset. I could only guess at who bought much of this stuff. It was possible to think of someone coming to buy, say, material and ribbons to stock their own shop elsewhere, but an individual casual shopper going away with a new pair of purple flip flops, a sack of flour, a Chinese lantern and a garishly-coloured plastic cat with a nodding head was, I suspect, a rarity.

Different areas have differing specialisations: in one place – Khlog Ong Ang Market – for toys, in others for electrical goods or car parts. If you visit Chinatown when other sights to note are the Holy Rosary Church, known as Kalawar Church (a corruption of Calvary) and famous for its stained glass windows showing scenes from *The Bible* dating from 1897; the art deco style building of Siam Commercial Bank; the Pathum Khongkha Temple, which is really old, dating way back to the Ayutthaya period. There are several temples, for instance Wat Mangkon Kamalawat, a large Mahayana Buddhist temple. More notable is Traimitwitthayaram Temple. These names don't really trip off the tongue and make asking for directions somewhat difficult, as pronouncing the name correctly is difficult if not impossible.

Chapter Three

The latter temple contains a Buddha image made from pure gold and weighing more than 5tons. It is said to be the largest gold figure in the world and was once covered with plaster to disguise the gold and avoid its theft by invaders. It seems safe enough now – it would hardly slip into a sneak thief's pocket and, indeed, moving it out of this warren of streets would surely now be well nigh impossible.

As I walked, the heat in the alleys soon became overpowering. So too did the need for a drink. There was not a Starbucks in sight, of course, even if I had wanted something so homogenised, but I did want some air conditioning. Back on the main road, I found a sizeable hotel with a small shopping arcade alongside in which there was a small café. I sat in the cool with an icy drink for a while before finding a taxi to take me back to my hotel. The driver spoke no English. I was hardly at the ends of the earth, but I was certainly not in an area that catered primarily for westerners. It was its own small world, within this great and now very cosmopolitan city.

The essentials of the market culture extend far beyond Bangkok and throughout the country. Tourists may find them fascinating but for the locals it is just a prime and convenient way to shop. Running a market stall, in town or village, is also how very many people make their living. Bartering for something small at a stall may be fun, as is getting a bargain, but you will never actually better anyone – they know their margins and will ensure there always is one.

Chapter Four

A LITTLE LUXURY

No useful distinction can be made between luxuries and necessities.
John Kenneth Galbraith

After a hot and hectic visit to a market, a bit of contrasting tranquillity may be necessary. If so, where better to take a moment than Bangkok's most famous hotel.

The Oriental was Bangkok's first large hotel and it opened in 1876. Since that time it has repeatedly been voted the best hotel in the world. Set on the side of the Chao Phraya River, it has a worldwide reputation and, amongst its many charms, afternoon tea in the famous Authors' Lounge amidst the potted palms and white wicker furniture, the place Somerset Maugham spent time recovering from malaria in the 1920's, is a real treat. Apart from staying there, something I have done a couple of times, many visitors must go just to see it and perhaps have a drink on the terrace at sunset, a meal or a coffee.

It is an iconic part of the scenery in Bangkok. Incidentally, not far away at the end of Silom Road is State Tower, a huge office block with a very stylish restaurant at the top. It is one of the tallest buildings in the city and the view, which takes in The Oriental, in daylight or at night, is spectacular. You can go up just for a drink, though a simple beer will cost you almost ten times the cost in the average bar. Or you can go up, have a sneaky look and leave discreetly and quickly before you have to buy anything. Or if you are as posh as it thinks it is, maybe you can afford a meal there and while away a pleasant evening (indeed, why not? I would like to think that I have some readers who could do so without blinking an eye). One warning: you have to be smartly dressed. I was once turned away for wearing a pair of sandals, even though they were smart ones and I was wearing neat slacks and a long sleeved shirt. Even your smartest jeans may be inadequate here and prompt a refused entry – *Oh no, sir, we can't let you in looking like a tramp who's fallen on hard times.* Actually they were very polite to me, but equally adamant.

Back to The Oriental.

It is one thing to experience an exceptional level of service, and the Oriental certainly delivers this with a style, grace and degree of friendliness that makes you feel spoiled almost to excess, but I wondered just what made it all possible. So on one of the two occasions on which I have stayed there, after breakfast I resolved to find out what the secret was. *What* turned out to be *who* and, given my interest, I was invited to take afternoon tea with two of The Oriental's key staff. I had heard tell of one of them, *Khun* Anakarna, on my last visit. In the year 2007 she celebrated working at the hotel for an extraordinary 60 years and it was a few more years until she retired. Even in 2012 she was still to be seen occasionally, popping in "to make sure all is okay". If I expected to meet someone broken down by the pressure of 60 years' hard work, I was very much mistaken. To say that Anakarna did not look her age is an understatement. She was poised, confident and altogether delightful; and looked immaculate in her beautiful silk outfit that was part and parcel of the way so many staff here are dressed.

With her was *Khun* Kaynee Nuengtawee who, as Executive Housekeeper, heads up a staff of more than 160 people all intent on ensuring that every room gives its occupants exactly what they want every day. She was, she said, "just a baby". By this it turned out that she meant that she had only worked for the hotel for 22 years. The hotel has a large proportion of long-serving staff and credits this with helping to guarantee that they are able to deliver the standard of service they intend. It must surely help.

How was the hotel's exceptional service delivered? Well, Kaynee was short on details, but certainly at pains to make clear that very little, if anything, was beyond them. There were tricks of course: notes were kept about guests so that someone could be offered their favourites. For instance, you might be asked if you wanted tea or coffee at your first breakfast, but on the second day what was offered first would be your choice of the day before. Some guests, those staying regularly and wanting things just so, would find everything in their room exactly as last time because, "we take a photograph to be sure that we can do this," Kaynee told me in a confidential tone.

After we had spoken for a little while, our tea arrived. My co-hosts teased the young waitress – something about her new eye make-up – and she giggled with them, but her delivery of the three different teas we had chosen and various scones, sandwiches and cakes was faultlessly executed. She returned periodically to top up our cups, hurrying forward the first time when I made to do this myself. Her smile lit up the already light and airy space of the famous Author's Lounge where we sat.

Many guests, as befits such an esteemed establishment I guess, stay a long time. Indeed, discussing this reminded me of the American I had spoken to on the Terrace earlier: his length of stay, described so matter-of-factly as spanning two months and involving six or seven weeks, had made me blanche at the cost that had to be involved. Such guests become well known to staff: they must be looked after and their return must be guaranteed. If any guest wants something to eat that is not on the menu, and not even in the hotel, then someone will run to the nearest market to buy it. Kaynee was very clear about their task.

"It is not magic," she said, "but it is our job to make the impossible possible – and because everyone feels the same and works together, the team can make anything happen." The right staff attitudes don't just happen, of course. Training is rigorous, but it is the instilment of the right attitude that my hosts made seem most important.

"We all know each other and work together as friends," said Kanee. This was a lady whom I quickly believed ran the tightest of ships. Yet there was every indication that it was their knowing how good they were and how highly guests rated them that gave every member of staff the incentive to excel.

Life in such a hotel is not without its problems, however. I was told two stories. First, about a regular guest who arrived and checked into his usual suite. Very soon he was on the phone demanding assistance. He had, he said, seen a lizard in the room. He hated them and was all set to check out unless the matter could be sorted. He was persuaded to give them some time and went off to a meeting as five of Kaynee's staff moved into the room in full hunting mode. I am not sure what this entailed: traps, rifles, nets, poison? It was probably not so dramatic, but they took the place apart, so to speak. No lizard, large or small was found – none.

"There was every likelihood that it had gone," Kaynee told me. "They hate the cold of an air conditioned room and it probably went out as we came in." But what was to be done? The guest was due back and there was no evidence of a captured lizard and a reptile free room to put his mind at rest. One of her people made a suggestion. He knew a garden nearby where there were lots of lizards. If they could capture one of the right colour then they could show it to the guest and all would be well. He was duly dispatched to catch a stand-in lizard and when the guest returned it was produced in a paper bag to persuade him to stay.

"He spent the next five days with us without any problem," said Kaynee. Problem solved, two lizards unharmed and a guest who felt he had been well looked after. Did Kaynee spend those days worrying, just in case the lizard had been well hidden, but reappeared? She said simply, "No." Bags of confidence and other matters to attend to I'm sure.

A second story described something rather different. Some years ago a guest came to Anakarna in the reading room off the Author's Lounge where she has her desk. He explained that he wanted to meet the kingdom's King and that he needed a fax sent at once to issue the invitation for the King to visit him in the hotel. It was quickly clear that he would brook no argument, and Anakarna had to go with him to a tiny nearby room from which, at the time, faxes were sent. As he became more and more strident and demanding she typed

Chapter Four

something out for him and sent it off to a number for a business in Bangkok which began with the words Royal House.

Not surprisingly, there was no instant reply, but Anakarna found she was virtually a prisoner with him as he insisted on her awaiting a reply that realistically she knew would never come. She had managed, on some pretext, to involve a colleague, so the three of them were shut in the tiny room. Agreeing to wait herself, she managed to send the colleague off on some contrived errand and, recognising the problem, he rang the phone in the room saying that there was an international call for the man, which he must take on another phone. He agreed to go to the desk to do so, and emerged into the arms of the by now waiting security staff. Although he was led away threatening to kill her, Anakarna finished the story by saying simply, "I don't think any other guests noticed at all". Never mind the inconvenience, and possible danger, to her, her concern was only for others. It takes all sorts. Given the time she has worked at the hotel, I suppose one encounter with a madman in 60 years is about par for the course.

More happily, she had recently been asked, not for the first time, to arrange a wedding for a regular guest. The hotel must play host to many weddings, but this was a small affair: a mature couple and just a dozen guests. Anakarna made the necessary arrangements, which included organising for someone to conduct the service and seeing to the various legalities for two people to marry away from their native land. She also arranged for the service to take place in the reading room, where she has her desk. This is a high-ceilinged room with the feeling of a grand library, which also contains a writing desk for guests and is lined with bookshelves. With everything ready, she was asked to take part in the ceremony and to give a reading. She had never been asked that before, but was happy to oblige. She dressed for the part. "I even managed to find a small silver cross to wear," she said. I cannot imagine anyone adding a greater sense of style and charm to such proceedings so effortlessly. I wish I had been there to see it.

Afternoon tea had been a delight. An hour and a half had sped by and I suddenly realised this, and worried about keeping these two from their many duties. If they were itching to get back to work, they politely showed no sign of it. However, we finished the last of our tea, I thanked them and we went our separate ways. Later, after my wife had checked in too (she was arriving later than me), a beautiful arrangement of flowers appeared in the bedroom with a note on it from *Khun* Kaynee wishing us well. Good service is obviously an absolute reflex for these two.

*

After my meeting with these two redoubtable ladies and as I went up the stairs from the lobby to the Business Centre on the Mezzanine floor to check my email, I passed the reception table for a large event being held in one of the conference rooms there. As the sign showed it was a British company, Friends Provident, I paused – perhaps nosily – to see what they were there for and I looked at the schedule posted publicly on an easel alongside the table. Now this is a major company in financial services, one I have had insurance policies with, indeed I have some shares in the company too,

Chapter Four

these having been offered to policyholders some years back at a special rate. In fact they are the only shares I have in a single individual company, so, small though my shareholding was, I wanted them to do well. Surely this was an extremely profligate use of their money to gather in such a hotel: and in a location that is hardly down the road from the city of London where they have their headquarters. What was it going to do to the price of my shares, I wondered? These, incidentally, have rarely gone above the price I paid for them and later dropped to an all-time low (which saw the company involved in a merger and acquisition that cost its shareholders dear).

Suddenly I was conscious of someone at my elbow. The lady at the desk had come up to see if she could help me. I asked what was going on and she told me that it was a gathering of their top sales people, a reward for their efforts and an incentive to future performance. It certainly looked like more reward than business. I was sure there would be *some* business element involved, if only to satisfy the taxman and ensure that any incentive was not negated by a hefty tax bill to cover the "benefit" of the jaunt. I remembered how on one occasion, wearing my business hat, I had been hired to speak at a weekend company conference in Majorca. I flew out on a plane full of families holding buckets and spades on which everyone applauded when the pilot landed safely, checked into the chosen hotel and presented myself at the designated conference room the following morning. It was empty. Eventually the organiser appeared and explained: "You didn't think you actually had to make a presentation, did you?" he said. "You just had to be on the programme to make the event tax deductible." Well, really! Still, once back in the U.K. I duly sent them an invoice and got paid my fee, and had a comfortable weekend on the terrace with a good book before I flew back.

Anyway, back to Friends Provident: the notice board showed that they had already visited the Grand Palace. "We had forty *tuk-tuks* lined up outside to bring people back to the hotel, all had a Friends Provident sign on them and we had a police escort across the city," she told me proudly. Well at least they were taking the opportunity to do some advertising as well as motivating the troops. She was wholly unfazed by my wondering out loud how the obviously high cost of the jaunt might affect my shares. "It's these people who keep the share value up," she said. "We have to look after them." Maybe, I thought, but must you do it here in quite so profligate a fashion? I decided not to argue; indeed, maybe she was correct.

The board showed that that evening they were going to experience Bangkok's famous Pat Pong Road night market. Here these financial whiz kids could have a drink or a meal unmolested, or they could visit bars of more dubious reputation if they wished, while returning to the hotel clutching some cheap T-shirts, fake jeans or pirated CDs and DVDs saying that they had "…only been shopping". Incidentally, should you go there, never buy DVDs of newly released films. At that early stage they will be filmed by hand in the cinema. The picture will be dark, the sound substandard and anyone who got up to go to the loo while the particular show was on will have the silhouette of their head immortalised blocking the picture as they move to and from the aisle.

Where in this playground would these pillars of the financial establishment go, I wondered. Maybe to bars from

Chapter Four

which the music blasts out into the street at a decibel level guaranteed to drown out any conversation inside and bring on deafness in later years for any regular customer. The scantily clad go-go dancers in such establishments still manage to entice in those uninterested in conversation or who kept the earplugs from the wash bag they will have got if they flew to Bangkok in the upper classes. Or to other bars where waitressing is only a side line for some of the hostesses, who will bring you a cold beer and want you to buy them a drink, but have their minds set on other business.

It was this scene that these financial hotshots were due to visit, and experience, that very evening. On the Friends Provident notice board, the word "experience" was in bold quotation marks and the notice made a visit to Pat Pong sound like a military expedition into hostile territory. There were dire warnings about the nature of some of the establishments that they might find there. Goodness me, the word sex appeared twice, and they were cautioned about being ripped off by unscrupulous bar owners tempting them in with scantily clad young ladies and then charging an amount for a drink equivalent to the gross national product of a small country. It made it sound as if they might have to sell some shares to extradite themselves. They were cautioned also not to miss the bus back, as "alternative transport might be hard to find". Well, actually not: a Skytrain station is two minutes' walk away and taxis ply for trade at both ends of the street all night long. The tone of the notice made being marooned there sound like a pretty high level hazard, when it was perhaps more likely that the worst that would occur, certainly to the men in the group, might be being persuaded to drink a sufficient amount in some bar to appear in the morning a little worse for wear. Now I thought about it, I rather hoped that those high flyers, responsible for boosting the value of my shares, might be just a tad more street smart than the apparent necessity for such a notice made them sound.

Later, back in England, I telephoned the company to see what they had to say about the event. I was promised a call back that was never made and phoned again, finally speaking to someone charged with dealing with the press. She did not know about the event – so obviously had not been invited – but however miffed she might be about that she promised that she would check and did phone me back later to confirm that I was correct, such an event had been held. Well, I *knew* that. She was equally robust about the expenditure, referring to "the competitive market" and saying that they had to match the staff benefits offered by their competitors. Further questions produced a very guarded response and the comment that she could say no more. So, there was clearly no question of me finding out what the event had cost, but I resolved to watch my share prices more closely in future (to no avail, as I have said). If you are ever scanning the appointments pages and see a job offering financial high flyers a good salary, pension, incentive payments and an annual visit to Bangkok's red light district, you will be able to make a good guess about which organisation is offering it.

The Oriental no doubt looked after them and their event superbly well, as they look after all their guests. The place is historic, iconic, in some ways cosmopolitan, yet also very Thai. It is an oasis in the concrete jungle and no one exploring Bangkok should fail to visit it.

Chapter Four

Chapter Five

FLOATING AWAY YOUR WORRIES

I am told it works even if you don't believe in it.
Scientist Neils Bohr (when asked if he believed
in the "lucky" horseshoe over his office door)

Most people have mixed feelings about travel; certainly you may have gathered that I have mixed feelings about it. So much of it is a pain, though I love to have travelled, and arriving somewhere you look forward to can be a pleasure that makes the memory of travel hassles quickly fade. Being in transit rarely makes one smile. It's dead time and if it is spent at an airport then, depending on the airport, it is either just tedious or hell on earth. If there is a little more time, if flight connections and arrangements allow, then it can be better. A nice hotel, a good meal and a chance to relax comfortably, and it becomes tolerable or even pleasurable. If your delay coincides with something special occurring then that is so much the better, and on one occasion that happened to me in Bangkok.

Thai is a difficult language to learn and its pronunciation defies the attempts of many to get their tongue around it. However there is one Thai word that it easy to say and which is worth explaining. *Sanuk* will usually be translated simply and literally as "fun". But it is much more than that: it is an enjoyment of life, of the moment, a putting aside of cares and a concentration on the occasion. The occasion may be something special, though that is not necessary. *Sanuk* best describes the enjoyment of those simple things in life that are pleasurable. It especially describes occasions involving friends and family, and that, of course, includes meals eaten in company and enjoyed together. Thais do not regard cooking and eating as refuelling. A meal, whatever it is, must be fun and this is as true of a snack from a mobile kitchen at the roadside as it is for something more formal. The food being good is important too, of course; it adds to the occasion.

Occasions come in all shapes and sizes.

Thailand has many festivals. *Songkran* is the Thai New Year and is celebrated in April. The principle activity, indeed an essential and boisterous one, is showering all and sundry with water. This is not just a few splashes, but can involve sizeable buckets! Beware if you go out that day; no one is safe. Other festivals include Buddha day – *Visakha Busha* – which marks the birth, enlightenment and death of the Buddha and is celebrated primarily around temples; The Royal Ploughing Ceremony, celebrated at the start of the rice planting season; and the Trooping the Colour on the King's birthday in December. There are also others as different as the Umbrella Fair held at Bo Sang and the Bun Bang Fai – Rocket Festival – held at Yasothon in northern Thailand to ensure sufficient rains. After the massive floods that swamped half of Thailand in November 2011, perhaps someone ought to give some thought to reducing the scale of this two-day festival, or at least toning down the revelry a little. Whoever did so, though, would no doubt be blamed for any subsequent drought.

Anyway, up and down the country it is any excuse for a festival, and whether it is a serious religious occasion or just a minor tradition, the concept of *sanuk* applies and means the same thing. It should be fun. Thais enter into all such festivities with gusto, which is why at their New Year you are not just likely to get a bit wet, but repeatedly soaked.

Back to my stopover: I had a couple of days. It was November. It was full moon and there was not just a festival due, but a major one. It was the Thai festival of *Loy Krathong*. The Thai words translate as floats (*loy*) and *krathong* means leaf cup. *Loy* is pronounced to rhyme with toy, *krathong* ends with a sound that, as so often with Thai words, I found impossible to get exactly right. To explain: the *krathong* is an offering floated on water – a *klong*, a river, lake or stream (even a flooded street) in homage to the goddess *Phra Mae Khongka* who oversees the wellbeing of waterways. This must be no frivolous task in a hot country where water is a precious commodity for agriculture and in life generally, though I do not expect that the goddess took on the responsibility of helping ensure hot tourists got a nice shower whenever they wanted.

I had heard of this event in the past but had never previously been in the country on the right day to experience it. So naturally I wanted to see what went on. I asked in the hotel and was told that, yes, people did get *krathong*, each one handmade on a bamboo frame from banana leaves and flowers to make a little floating tribute, most often, I discovered later, in a shape reminiscent of a birthday cake, and throughout Bangkok they did go to the waterside to garner good luck by putting them into the river or a *klong* and letting them float away. My informant made the whole event

Chapter Five

sound pretty low key, but that notwithstanding, I set off for the river a little after darkness had fallen to see for myself what went on.

Outside the hotel the traffic was, as so often, horrendous. It was still rush hour with a vengeance. I watched for several minutes and nothing moved at all in either direction. I then consulted a lady at the taxi desk by the entrance, who not only suggested the sky train, which had a station 10 minutes' walk away on Silom Road, and stopped at a pier on the river, but said she was on her way there and offered to walk with me. Usually Bangkok's sky train is hugely efficient: quick, convenient and air-conditioned, it glides above the busy streets and makes otherwise difficult journeys easy. We only wanted to go three stops, my new friend Yip bought the tickets, and we waited for a train, positioning ourselves carefully alongside where the doors would open. The platforms are marked, and when a train arrives it stops with great precision with its doors exactly where they are indicated to be. It seems to speak of pretty good driving, but is actually only the result of some clever little microchip and a computer programme that actually works.

The next train arrived promptly and to say it was packed was an understatement. A wall of people bulged out in relief as the doors opened, rather as if the carriage itself was exhaling. One couple did disembark, squeezing through those standing nearer to the door than them. Yip unhesitatingly elbowed her way in and I followed, with her assuring me that we "must get on" as "the next train no better. Worse." Then *"Loy Krathong* very important," she said by way of explaining the crowds. Not so low key then.

The train made slow progress and kept stopping between stations but eventually it reached Taksin Pier and most passengers got off. Down the stairs we all went and it was quickly apparent that the area at the bottom and around the pier was solid with people. At tables along the way towards the water, stallholders sold beautifully constructed *krathong* in various sizes. There must have been thousands of them; contemplating how many people were involved in making the huge number presumably used nationwide made the mind boggle. I bought one, and one for Yip too, and we struggled along amidst the sea of people to the riverside, where we both added a coin to our float – this being an important final touch if you were to receive good luck, she explained."Only little money, big luck, no problem."

We effected a successful launch and watched as our offerings bobbed away on the currant, quickly losing sight of them amongst the many thronging the river, launched both from this pier and upstream. It is traditional to make a wish. So I did, though it is traditional, too, not to tell anyone what it is. People at the river's edge were equipped and ready to light the sticks of incense and candles that topped the *krathongs* and the smoke and light from these showed far out into the river. On the edge of the river, making a launch meant leaning out over the water from a floating metal pier that bobbed energetically and erratically, both from the movement of the river below and from the crowd of moving people on top. There were some awkward moments; I heard some shouts and screams followed by laughter, but no one actually fell in. Far from being low key, the festival seemed to be bringing a major proportion of Bangkok's population to

Chapter Five

the riverside. The chatter of happy voices filled the night air and it was clear that everyone looked forward to the event.

From this particular pier, courtesy boats operate ferrying people to and from various hotels along the river to the sky train station. The boat from the Anantara was just docking and I bid Yip farewell; having made her offering she was off home. "Work all day, now cook all evening," she said, listing numerous family members who had to be fed. The crowd swallowed her behind me and I jumped on the boat resolving to have supper by the river and see what a riverside hotel was doing to mark the occasion. It was a relief to get out of the crush of people; good natured though the crowd had been, and though the number of boats on the river seemed much greater than usual, I had a quiet half hour to spend with the lights of the city ranged around me and reflecting on the water as the boat picked its way down river with a host of *krathong* floating all around it. The boat was quite crowded too: a disparate group of people, some no doubt hotel guests and some too, like me, using the boat to give them a (free) view of the festivities. A Thai family spanning several generations sat in a group around the stern, the children chattering excitedly about the festivities and watching everything around them. Overhead, another sign of the festival, hot air paper-lanterns two to three feet high were carried serenely along by the breeze, rising higher and higher, pushed by the hot air generated by the burner beneath them. The children lent out from under the awning of the boat, craning their necks and pointing.

I was at the front of the boat and when the single crew member (in addition to the helmsman) had dished out cold towels to everyone he sat down near me. I asked about the significance of the festival and got a potted history. There is no one story about it. Its origin is lost in the mists of time. Some say it originated in India. Whatever the origin was, it is largely forgotten and Thais young and old –obviously a great many of them – regard it simply as *sanuk*.

Away from the cities the link with water is stronger; the festival is very much a thank you for the gift of water so important to farming, and in the modern world some regard it as an act of remission for the pollution of so much of it. Maybe that is one of the motivations in Bangkok, where many *klongs* can make the average sewer seem clean. Actually, the river and canals are much cleaner than they used to be; sewage treatment may be rudimentary by some standards, but there are fish in the river three feet long. It is said it is an ideal murderer's river – any body dumped in it does not last long. One still sees plenty of kids swimming in the *klongs*, they jump from bridges and generally seem to enjoy themselves, though I have heard locals say cynically that they are not really swimming – "just going through the motions".

Another possible origin for the festival stems, unsurprisingly in so Buddhist a country, from a tale about the Lord Buddha. At the Mammada River, a naga, which is a mythical snake, asked the Buddha to leave a footprint on the bank as an image that could be worshipped after he had gone. He did so, though there is no written confirmation of the story to link it more firmly to the festival. The timing at least is clear: Loy Krathong takes place at the end of the 12th lunar month, just as the three months of most intensive rice planting is finished. Farmers rest after their exertions, the rains ease as weather improves and the growing season begins; the next harvest is just one month away.

Chapter Five

Floating lanterns have been known in some places, especially the ancient city of Sukhothai, for more than 700 years. "Why so?" I asked several Thais and all replied the same way: "It's fun". Well, so it is. But that's not all. A lady, Nang Nopphamas, the daughter of a priest in the King's court in the late 1200s, is said to have witnessed the King picnicking on the canals as part of celebrations in homage to Phra Mae Khongkha, goddess of waterways. Feeling that a picnic was insufficient as a celebration she made the first *krathong* in the shape of a lotus flower with lighted candles and incense sticks on top. She floated this towards the King who accepted it as gift and agreed that it added enchantment to the occasion. What the King does one day, the population does the next; well, not quite perhaps, but such a tale does seem a likely start for the tradition now universally observed.

Some celebrations, certainly those in Sukhothai and the north of the country, include beauty pageants to choose a modern Nang to preside over the proceedings. There is a romantic aspect to all this too: if a couple launch a *krathong* together and the light on it survives the elements for a good while, it shows that their love will endure. That sounds a bit hazardous: it surely should not blight a burgeoning love if the *krathong* jointly launched is swamped by an inconsiderate ferry on a busy river. Whatever the truth of all this, *Loy Krathong* is now a regular part of Thai life and I was lucky to be there on the right day to see it.

When the boat reached the hotel I saw that a large, low, flat, barge-like vessel had been tied up to the small jetty to provide people with a gathering place and somewhere from which to launch their *krathongs*. The hotel has a nightly barbeque on a terrace by the riverfront, followed by a display of traditional Thai dancing. Tonight it would end with a parade for the diners to launch their *krathongs*, these presumably provided by the hotel.

I had some supper in a small café on the ground floor alongside the gardens and the hotel pool. Always a pleasant spot, there were few people in it that night, most guests perhaps having opted to pay for the big dinner or gone elsewhere. A small card on the table told me that there were due to be fireworks at 10 o'clock, and I finished a pleasant meal a little before that time and went to get a cold beer by the river. I have some traditions of my own and one is that Thai food is always best accompanied by a cold *Singha*. Promptly at 10 o'clock I heard music and a small band led the diners from the large open air restaurant to the jetty. As the first people arrived, hotel staff acting as helpers came forward to light the candles and incense and help get their *krathongs* on their way. They all carried long bamboo poles with wire mesh baskets on the end. These were each loaded with a *krathong* and dipped carefully into the water, letting it float free and sending it on its way without extinguishing the candles; all very organised. I just hoped that they remembered to remind people to add the coin which Yip had assured me was essential to prompting good luck. I might be 10 *baht* worse off, but I was certainly having a good evening, so maybe it had worked. Or was working; I had neglected to ask how quickly results might be expected. The front of the queue reached the water's edge just as the fireworks began. There had been a few visible earlier elsewhere up and down the river, but the Anantara really went to town – loud, high, dramatic and beautiful, they continued for at least 20 minutes, and the display ended in a spectacular crescendo of

Chapter Five

high, brightly coloured, overlapping cascades with new showers of falling stars appearing as each bang echoed across the sky.

To return to my own hotel I decided not to repeat my boat journey and fight my way back through the crowds no doubt remaining at the pier by the river and on the sky train, but to get a taxi. Surely the traffic would have died down by late evening. It had, but it was still busier than usual. The journey back meant crossing the river, the huge, high bridge, normally the domain only of six lanes of traffic, was packed with people from end to end. As everyone was positioned to either side looking out over the river, there remained space of sorts for my taxi and other traffic to thread its way through in the centre. But for the moment at least, people had clear priority over traffic.

So, *Loy Krathong* is certainly not low key. It is an important festival and one that involves many people from all walks of life, whether because of the old legends or just because it is fun. It had been fun for me too, spellbinding if a little hectic; I would love to see a ceremony in some quieter part of the country on another occasion – though quite where it would be quieter I'm not sure. This is a large festival everywhere: in Chiang Mai, where it takes place a day earlier and has the name *Yee Peng*, so many lanterns are set soaring skywards that it creates a hazard to aircraft. Being Thailand, there is not a restriction on the lanterns, but flights above are suspended for the duration. "Of course," I was once told, "You can't have a festival, *sanuk*, and a chance to prompt some good luck hindered by a few flights. They wait."

All this was followed by good news. The following morning the newspapers reported that the Thai King, whose health had not been so good and had just had a spell in hospital, was sufficiently well to have gone to the river to personally participate in the ceremony. This was universally regarded as a good sign, not just because the King is held in such affection, but because it is also reckoned that the volatile Thai political situation will not be helped when he dies. Realistically – he is in his 80s – this is a possibility that could be not so far off given his ill health. Meantime I would like to think that it was the good luck emanating from all those coins floating down river and on water throughout the country that had helped get him sufficiently mobile to take part. Maybe my few *baht* had just made the difference.

My transit break over, later that morning I checked in for my flight home. After the usual security checks and a while waiting, when I got to the gate I was upgraded from economy to business class – a vanishingly rare and totally inexplicable event. Maybe there really is something in this *Loy Krathong* good luck business; certainly I had a comfortable flight. It seemed that my ten *baht* was very well spent. And besides, the wish I had made might still come true.

Chapter Five

Chapter Six

DON'T HOLD YOUR BREATH

He who is drowned is not troubled by rain.
Chinese proverb

Thailand is a large country so there are plenty of possibilities for excursions. Visiting the elephants was one trip that certainly made me smile, and another excursion led to my doing something I had never done before. This involved subjecting myself to the uncertainties of another flight, a short internal one on this occasion. I was off to an island. All went smoothly; there were even some smiles along the way – I must be careful or I'll be finding travelling pleasurable next.

After checking in, I went through security. Passengers' cabin baggage was being x-rayed and a young lady in front to me set off the alarm. Her case – bright pink and on wheels – was opened and, despite most people having got used to the current regulations about not carrying liquids, the contents of her case seemed to consist of little other than gels and liquids. The security officer lined up the offending items one by one in a long row. It included shampoo, body lotion, sun protection cream, moisturiser and a plethora of other potions, the purpose of which I could only guess at. Whatever was in them, the aerosols, pots and bottles all seemed to be pastel shades. When maybe 20 or so bottles stood side by side in a row, he suggested very politely that she should return to check-in and let the bag go in the hold. I could not

Chapter Six

understand her reply and don't know if it contained an explanation for her lapse; maybe she was a first time traveller or had lived on another planet for a while and the level of present day security was a mystery to her. In any case, she finally retreated, suitably chastened and the security man waved me forward with a raised eyebrow and an apology for the delay. He didn't actually say, "Some people are unbelievable," but he looked as if he was thinking it.

Landing at *Koh* Samui's tiny airport is like landing in a garden and going back in time. Beautiful flowers line the runway and surround the terminal building, which is small and without walls. The "buses" that bring passengers from the aircraft to the terminal consist of open-sided trucks that reminded me of toys. Each has a trailer. But it all works: even the antiquated carousel rattling and shaking round in a loop succeeded in bringing my suitcase safely from the bowels of the plane and reuniting me with it in good time. The plane had, however, departed from Bangkok late. No explanation had been volunteered for this; but I expect some schedule-crippling event had occurred – perhaps one of the stewardesses had broken a finger nail at a crucial moment. As a result, I emerged into the airport an hour or so after I had planned to do so. My journey did not end there. I still had to get to another, smaller island and went to the information desk to ask about the ferry. The girl behind the counter was helpfulness personified, but still she smilingly told me that having missed the one o'clock ferry I had been aiming for, there would not be another one for four hours. Her smile remained in place throughout her "I know it's not what you want to hear, but there's nothing you can do about it – so what the heck" message. Other passengers were in the same position; a small group of us grumbled together as travellers do, but the consensus was that it was probably better to wait at the port rather than at the airport. That way we would at least have the illusion of making some immediate progress.

As we moved out of the building, we were momentarily blinded by the hot sun, then went in search of a taxi. A taxi here meant a *baht* bus: a pick-up truck with seats along the open sides, no meter and definitely no air conditioning. The driver, a youth wearing jeans and a grubby T-shirt bearing some indecipherable words in Thai, quoted us a price. With four hours to get to the harbour we could take our time haggling, even though the fare was to be shared between four of us and the cost would be very little. In the course of this debate, the driver discovered our situation and changed tack.

"You want express boat," he said, with the tone of one uttering a profound truth. "Boat go in half an hour." He explained that the ferry did not have a monopoly, a variety of other services operated and he knew one that would whisk us to *Koh* Phenang, the island I was actually to visit, in a matter of moments. Having some experience of Thailand, it did not surprise me that this had not been mentioned at the airport desk, after all no one had asked about other services and their job was to sell ferry tickets. I was happy to give this "express boat" a try, and my fellow travellers also agreed. A new price was agreed and we piled into the back of the truck and pulled away in a cloud of dust.

I sat next to an Indian girl in her mid-20s. Usha was on her first visit to Thailand and was finding the uncertainties that had suddenly been introduced into her carefully planned journey somewhat worrying and unwelcome.

Chapter Six

After 15 minutes of bumpy driving, we pulled up not at the port, but alongside a small, undistinguished pier. One of a couple of adjacent buildings sold tickets for the "express boat" and also supplied a cold drink, which the heat was already making a necessity. The boat was due to depart in "10 minutes". Thai time is famously uncertain and has a subtle and mysterious elasticity. People will arrange an appointment for say 11 am and stroll in at 12.30 without a hint of an explanation or even an apology. This cultural quirk stems in part from the notorious Bangkok traffic, indeed when setting an appointment people will say, "Make it 11 am – Bangkok time." by way of acknowledgement that this happens. So I knew that this particular 10 minutes might mean anything from 10 minutes to a couple of hours, but on this occasion, happily, it proved actually to mean 10 minutes.

We were soon led from the ticket counter to the end of the pier where a further small group of prospective travellers was already gathered, standing together around a pile of luggage. It was a mixed group ranging from young backpackers to older holidaymakers and local people. Below the pier, invisible, perhaps 12 feet down until we approached close enough to see, was our boat.

Probably not more than 25-foot long, it was not a solid boat but a large inflatable rubber zodiac. Inside, the floor was boarded, in the centre was a steering wheel and at the back an outboard motor the size of a small car. The owner and skipper began throwing the bags and suitcases down to his young assistant who arranged them in an untidy heap in the bow and covered them, in a rudimentary fashion, with a well-worn green tarpaulin. It had sufficient holes in it to make the description "waterproof" inappropriate. Then the passengers, ominously there were 13 of us, were invited to scramble down some stone steps and sit – cling would be a better word – in a semi-circle around the stern half of the boat behind the helmsman. This was accomplished with some trepidation. The inflated rubber boat flexed and lurched as passengers stepped on.

Usha initially refused to board and demanded the return of her bag, fare and peace of mind. Eventually the difficulties of changing her mind and finding her bag coupled with the encouragement of others – "it is the quickest way" – had her relenting. She gingerly made her way down the steps and, clad in bulky life jackets, passed round once we were seated, we all awaited departure. The skipper surveyed the faces around him. Usha was still clearly miserable. Several others looked a touch uneasy at finding themselves a mere few inches from the surface of the water and were no doubt wondering, as I confess was I, if it would have been better to wait for the more substantial sized ferry. The skipper ignored all signs of reservation and launched into a formal welcome. "Right everyone, to island take about 12 to 15 minutes," he said brightly. "Hang on tight." Then he went into airline mode and continued, "Please note the emergency exits, they're… well, all round you really, but it calm today – we go now." He grinned: he had doubtless seen nervous passengers before.

The large engine rumbled into life and we began to move away from the jetty at a comfortable pace. Fifty metres out he pushed the throttle hard forward, the bow of the boat lifted and we set off as if intent on a place in the Guinness Book of Records – though whether the record was to be for the fastest island hop or the most frightened passengers was a moot point. Actually, although the boat seemed to leap from wave to wave, the bow hitting each wave with a loud slap, the sea was pretty calm and with minimal spray coming over the side it quickly became an invigorating journey. The island ahead of us grew rapidly in size, rather, it occurred to me, as anyone going overboard would diminish in size in the wake, and soon 12 minutes had passed and we were slowing and pulling alongside another small jetty. By this time anyone with a milky drink in their bag was probably transporting cheese.

"Good time, good time," advised our skipper, as someone appeared on the jetty above to secure us and a rope snaked from boat to quay. Bearing in mind that the ferry takes about 50 minutes to reach the island, and that seems to go at a pretty good pace, we must have been moving at a fair old lick.

As the passengers scrambled up a vertical, rickety steel ladder about two metres high, bags were sent flying up from the boat to be laid out in a line along the jetty. Working for the express boat clearly gave you strong arms. Usha had a jumbo-sized rucksack that was caught less than cleanly and nearly tumbled back. Yet to scramble up the steps, she was watching this from within the boat and, for a second, as her bag teetered on the brink of a watery fate and the catcher laughed like a maniac and grinned from ear to ear, her face registered abject horror. My suitcase safely on dry land, I watched this from the jetty, congratulating myself on the small triumph of swapping a long wait for a unique crossing and four more hours on the island. Usha was the last person up the steps, muttering, "I'm getting the ferry back, I'm getting the ferry back," like a mantra as she got her feet back safely on solid ground. Our skipper grinned again and waved to his next group of intrepid passengers moving down the jetty to join the next run.

Everyone was going off in different directions now, many of the younger passengers set on attending the full moon party. This was, logically enough, a beach party held on the island at every full moon. The event – due in a couple of days – has become internationally well known and must be responsible for a goodly amount of the tourism here. I am not sure why it has become so well known. It basically consists of a large crowd milling about on a stretch of beach while local people play enormously loud music at them and sell them rudimentary food and lots of beer while huge bonfires blaze. The most notable happening seems to be the fire rope, but that is just a long rope soaked in something that can be set on fire and used for skipping. Maybe it looks dramatic in the dark and after a few bottles of the local *Singha* beer. Anyway, everyone grabbed their luggage and went off to find transport to their respective accommodation. The resort that I had booked proved to be about half an hour distant. It was a journey that quickly showed the nature of the island to be much less developed than is the case on *Koh Samui* itself and my *baht* bus made its way along fairly basic roads and past simple village houses and shops.

I was quickly made welcome at the Green Papaya resort, a collection of about 20 rooms constructed in a semi-circle of villas facing the sea. The pool at its centre was long and ended with a horizon edge that looked down on the beach and out to sea. The restaurant, set above the sand, was to prove excellent. Though there were cheaper places around, this was both reasonable and good. The hotel had been recommended by the scuba diving school, the reason for my visit, at which I was due in the morning, and which was

Chapter Six

located sufficiently close for anyone going there to be collected first thing for their day out.

Having unpacked, sorted myself out and had a swim to give me a stretch after the journey, I wandered down to the restaurant and sat above the beach, a small horseshoe-shaped cove a few hundred metres across and, as I found looking out across the beach to the sea, facing the sunset. Soon after six o'clock the light began to change. Not much more than an hour or so later it was dark. To say that the time in between afforded a dramatic view would be like saying Attila the Hun was a bit of a rogue. The sunset was truly awesome: a calm sea, an array of small fishing boats coming and going, and above it all enough small clouds to ensure a light show of special effects proportions. Every moment the appearance of the sky seemed to change in a profusion of colour, red, orange and mauve, and any single moment would have yielded a snapshot of prize-winning quality as the ball of the sun sank slowly behind the clouds and below the horizon. It was a quiet spot too, so all this was accompanied by little more than the sound of tiny waves breaking on the sand.

I was so mesmerised that my beer got neglected and became warm – a disaster easily remedied by ordering another as the last of the light faded and darkness and a wonderful array of stars took over until the morning. Later, I stepped down to the beach and walked a little way into virtually total darkness to see the stars in a way that light pollution in most places makes impossible. It was not only the view that was good, a smiling waitress soon had an excellent meal in front of me and I retired to bed replete.

I had telephoned Lotus Diving during the afternoon and confirmed my booking, made on the internet a while back.

They were expecting me and would pick me up at 8.30 in the morning for my first scuba diving lesson. Now it was imminent, the prospect of my underwater jaunt began to seem somewhat daunting. I had never done this before and wondered quite why I wanted to do it now.

The idea had begun with some poolside eavesdropping a few months previously. I overheard someone being briefed about a diving trip, and my ears pricked up on hearing sharks being mentioned. It got my attention because they were being mentioned as an attraction. Not "This is how we avoid coming within a thousand miles of a shark"; more, "Lucky you, you've a good chance of seeing some reef sharks. Up close. Sorry they are not likely to be very large, maybe only two metres long." That must make their mouths big enough to… no, I didn't want to go there.

"There's no feeding of sharks here," said the instructor, "so they don't associate people with food." Well, there's a relief, I thought. Although surely this meant that they would eat you if they realised you were tasty, but apparently and luckily it hadn't dawned on them. Well. Not. Yet. The instructor was conducting short "taster" sessions in the pool and I had a go; it whetted my appetite.

Certainly the incident had set me thinking and on, the basis that most things should be tried at least once, I had done a little research and contacted the diving school. An exchange of emails had then quickly persuaded me that it was something I "just had to do" and the arrangements had been made.

The following morning a pickup truck from the dive school arrived as promised and I was off. Once there, I joined a group of four other novices and the first stage was being talked through the process while still firmly on dry land. I

Chapter Six

suppose that being 12 metres under water is inherently dangerous, unless you're a fish, and even for fish it's dangerous unless you are near the top of the food chain and have developed good avoidance techniques for hooks, nets and bigger or toothier fish.

I was impressed with the thoroughness with which everything was done. It was clear that no one was going to get even a toe wet until they understood the basic principles. It was encouraging, too, that payment was not due until the end of the course; was it right to presume that money was only due if you survived? If I drowned it might leave a little more cash for the funeral.

The briefing over and having wriggled into a wet suit, I soon found myself at the bottom of an extra deep swimming pool with an air tank on my back and a regulator in my mouth. Vic, for five years an instructor at Lotus Diving, had kitted me up with all the gear. With extreme patience and meticulous instruction, he and his fellow instructor Gem, got me breathing underwater – "breathe continuously and never hold your breath." Right. I breathed successfully. It all felt a little weird, but it did work. But then they changed tactics and apparently became intent on drowning me, cheerfully insisting that I drop my regulator (that, should you not know, is the gadget that you put in your mouth to breathe from). I had to retrieve it and also, another test, I had to flood my facemask with water and was then shown how to clear it if (when?) this happened accidentally. It was all somewhat unnerving, especially as instructions as to what to do were given above the surface and seemed to evaporate from my mind entirely the second I went under water.

Nevertheless, having survived the first stage, I learnt some sign language. I concentrated firmly on the one indicating "I've got a problem". More were added and soon I knew how to signal left, right, up and down as well as ask for help. Gem also showed me the sign for "okay", made with the index finger forming a circle with the thumb; to avoid underwater misunderstandings, this one presumably needs varying internationally, as in a number of countries, including Brazil, such a gesture is obscene.

Next day, after a pleasant 45-minute journey out to sea in the school's two tier boat, a vessel about 40 feet long with a dry deck upstairs and a wet deck below from which people went into the sea, the boat dropped anchor in a spot carefully chosen so that the anchor did no damage to the reef. We all kitted up. Then I found myself standing, ungainly in all the equipment, on a platform at the stern of a boat with my designated Thai instructor for the day, Gem, saying, "Hold regulator and face mask with one hand, weight belt with other – and take big step."

Amazing myself, I did. The bright green water enveloped me. Zion, another of the Lotus team, guided me down the anchor rope, signing to me to equalise the pressure as I went by blowing through my nose to clear my ears, rather as you do in an aeroplane. Dire warnings that without this I would die horribly ensured that I did just that. I even managed to signal okay to him at the same time. Then I was 12 meters down and in another world. The water was clear and the only sound I could hear was my own regular breathing; the words "breath continuously" buzzed in my brain. Despite some prior apprehension, at this stage I found the feeling was amazing. If I did nothing I hung unmoving in the water.

Chapter Six

Moving took little effort: just a few kicks with the flippers sent me forward. Everywhere, brightly coloured fish swam in profusion: from tiny, fiercely territorial clown fish, defending their young from vastly larger creatures and divers, to huge grouper, maybe not two-metre shark length, but decidedly big and mean-looking from my perspective. I learned only later that grouper are particularly friendly and like having their stomachs tickled by divers in the manner of a dog. Schools of fish cruised amidst the rocks, moving in unison. Sea anemones extended waving fingers and giant clams kept silent watch amongst the coral. I think I saw sponges too, reminding me of the teasing question of how much higher sea levels around the world would be if sponges didn't exist.

Nearly an hour went by as if it were maybe 10 minutes. I gradually found that breathing needed less conscious thought and I could concentrate more on the view and profusion of life around me. All too soon, we surfaced right by the boat. I pushed on the right button to inflate my BCD (Buoyancy Control Device: the jacket housing all the breathing gear) and paddled towards the boat's ladder. Removing my flippers, my underwater weightlessness disappeared and I struggled up the steps. I sat to shed the heavy air tank and weight belt. My belt seemed very heavy having had a little extra weight added to it, explained by the cheerful comment, "Fat floats" from the delectable Gem, who was waif thin and made a wetsuit look like the most stylish outfit in her wardrobe.

The next day I did it again. Perhaps it's not for everyone. One of my small group, a young American on holiday from university, managed only half of one dive, and evidently surfaced saying, "Never again". He did not return for the second day. On day two, even if I did not feel quite like an old hand, the experience was less strange. Again I took my "big step" off the stern of the boat, this being necessary to ensure that the air tank on your back does not hit the boat behind you as you drop into the water.

The water was again very clear, the view mesmerising. One of the things I saw again was a clown fish, a small brightly coloured fish. What was, I think, a mother and babies swam at the fringe of a coral outcrop, the babies sheltered within the waving arms of an anemone. As I approached the little fish, which was no more than six inches long, it charged me. It had no armament and posed no threat, but it literally rushed at me repeatedly as I approached. I imagined it saying, "No closer, not one flip closer or I call my friend the reef shark," before it finally dropped back as I went by. I was later told that clown fish are one of the most territorial and aggressive fish in the sea; though their size prevents them having much effect on the likes of a diver, they certainly act to protect their family and do not seem to take much account of size differences.

At one point, we encountered a current. It was sufficiently strong to raise some sand and debris from the sea bottom as our little group swam against it for a minute or two. It produced an odd effect: as I watched the divers nearest to me, they appeared to be swimming at enormous speed, their motion exaggerated by the stream of bits apparently rushing past them. Soon we were past its influence and tranquillity returned. The underwater world continued to fascinate: the colours, the many fish and the sheer feeling of gliding through an alien environment so effortlessly made it worth all the travel and arrangements. In all I did four dives, each

Chapter Six

approaching one hour in duration. I did not grow fins but I began to feel more fish-like.

All too soon, my last dive was over and I was back on board divesting myself of the scuba kit. In due course, the dive boat made its way back to the island from the smaller island, the shores of which we had again moored by. After a pleasant voyage I took stock of my experience. The American student may not have liked it, but me, I think I'm hooked – at least until I see a shark. My dives to date had been mercifully free of them, even though I hadn't actually specified the no-shark option as I didn't want to be a wuss. Why ever didn't I do this many years ago? When can I do it again? If you travel somewhere suitable – and Thailand is ideal – and can take a few days, have a go.

As I took my leave, it was clear that all those working at the school were not just expert and enthusiastic, but drew great satisfaction from introducing others to a pastime about which they were passionate. They were lucky enough to work doing something they clearly loved, and loved it also when others discovered and enjoyed their passion. Everyone smiled as I left, Gem accompanying hers with the invitation, "Come again, anytime". It's a thought; maybe one day I will.

Chapter Seven

SO SORRY, WE'RE CLOSED

Last week, I went to Philadelphia, but it was closed.
W. C. Fields

Not everything in the land of smiles immediately makes you smile. The unique character of the place is a delight, but aspects of the culture can create problems too. The quotation above from the old-time American comedian W. C. Fields was a remark intended to insult. Philadelphia, he implied, was boredom in bricks and mortar – a town so mind-numbingly uninteresting that, as far as a visitor was concerned, it might as well have been closed. You may think that this is a sentiment that could well be applied to many a town – take your pick. But there are occasions when such a remark can be taken more literally.

Years ago in Britain, many, perhaps most, towns had an early closing day once a week when shops closed at lunchtime and in the afternoon the place took on the appearance of a ghost town: lone dogs populated whole streets, parking places were empty and litter blew unimpeded along the pavements rather as those round bundles of dried grass – tumbleweed – did in old-fashioned Western movies. The sleepy seaside resort where I was brought up was pretty quiet on a normal day; on half-day closing day it was as if everybody had been wiped out by a plague – even the sea was uncharacteristically quiet and the normally noisy seagulls whispered.

Chapter Seven

These days our cities never sleep; we talk about 24/7 and expect to be able to buy anything from a pizza to a piano at three o'clock in the morning as easily as we do between nine and five. This is all doubtless very useful, I mean imagine 5am without pizza, it's unthinkable. But all this does come with a downside: never ceasing traffic noise, shops and offices lit around the clock, the power they need adding to our already dangerous carbon emissions, and constant hustle and bustle blighting the lives of many people just wanting a quiet night's sleep. So used are we to this situation nowadays that if any town or city were to close for even a short while, it would be seen as truly remarkable. Maybe I should lay in more pizza just in case.

But maybe it really could happen. And imagine not only a town being closed, but a whole country. This is effectively what did happen to Thailand at the end of November 2008. It closed. Not for an hour or an afternoon, but for some 10 whole days. Or rather, its main airports did, and that's lockdown enough. Tens of thousands of people, locals, tourists and business visitors alike, were stuck in the country unable to depart. Similarly, in a country where the largest industry is tourism, none of the visitors due to arrive could do so – they, and their money, stayed at home. Many Thais were also marooned overseas and unable to return to work and family. How did this come to occur? Thailand's unfathomable politics is complex, and I suspect that any Thai word there may be for Machiavellian conveys about twice the normal level of chicanery as it does elsewhere. This is no political guide, so suffice to say that supporters of one of the main political parties, feeling that the government was too closely linked to the recently discredited and ousted Prime Minister Thaksin, began a series of demonstrations.

So far, so normal; protests occur in every country and there are perhaps few, if any, nations where politicians are truly popular. After a variety of gatherings, protesters then hit on the idea of assembling at Bangkok's main airport. Suvarnabhuma is a new airport, at that time it had only opened a year or so ago and had been built in expectation of consolidating Thailand's position as South East Asia's main hub, a goal that was about to be dealt a knock-out blow. No one actually put a "Closed" sign on the door, but with several thousand people – all wearing the protesters' trademark yellow shirts – assembled along the outside drop-off point and in the check-in area within the terminal, and with the access road blocked with traffic, the airport authorities rapidly decided to close the airport, declaring that operations were not viable. Staff disappeared on an ad hoc holiday leaving intending passengers to their own devices. Bangkok's old airport, Don Muang, used mainly for domestic flights, was also closed in a similar way.

All this started slowly. No one, I suspect, passengers, officials or government believed for an instant that the closure would last long – a few hours, a day or two at most. How could it be more? Official reassurances were issued, confidently stating that everything would be back to normal "very soon".

It wasn't.

A week went by. Further days passed. And it was 10 long days before the country opened again. Now let's be clear about this. The demonstration certainly involved a large number of people, but quite quickly the press around the

Chapter Seven

world began to report all this in very strong terms: Thailand was painted as a lawless and dangerous place; people in many countries found their governments and travel industries issuing heavy warnings about the advisability of going there. And, to be fair, there were a few isolated incidents of violence around the country, mainly near government buildings, but the gathering at the airport was essentially peaceful and in the rest of the country the sun shone, life simply went on as normal and no change was detectible. As someone in the southern resort town Hua Hin told me, "Protest, it's not really a protest, just a small traffic problem".

No one made any attempt to stop the demonstrators going to the airport and, apart from some half-hearted requests for people to leave, no real attempt was made to shift them. In fact, official responses never got visibly heavier than saying "please leave". The local newspapers mentioned constant meetings of officials and ministers, and talk, not action, seemed to be the order of the day. Nowhere were there the water cannon, tear gas, transparent shields and the like that are produced by the police in, say London, Paris or Barcelona at the mere hint of any trouble. Police attended, of course, and for the most part chatted amicably to the demonstrators.

At one point, when police numbers were increased somewhat in a show of strength, demonstrators and police actually lined up facing each other in front of the terminal while, in an almost party-like spirit, one small group of demonstrators crept round behind the police line and let all their car tyres down. They might have been unruly school children. As I read about this, the line from the Monty Python film *Life of Brian* came to mind, "He's a very naughty boy", but this naughtiness, it had to be remembered, was adversely affecting a very large number of people.

As the duration of the closure lengthened things also became more fluid. People came and went from the airport, again with no attempt being made to stop this happening. Many people spent a couple of days at the demonstration, then went back to their family or business to keep ordinary life on the go, and returned a day or two later. Many of those there were women. There were also large numbers of children of all ages present. People brought camp beds, cooking equipment, and bands and dancers mixed with the crowds to keep people happy. There was in part a party atmosphere, mingled with a sense of optimism. No comment reported from the protesters seemed to allow for any possibility other than that they would achieve their aims.

Despite this atmosphere, the effect of such a long closure was devastating to travellers, the airport's business and all associated tourist attractions. Gradually, as marooned people managed to slip away, overland or by circuitous routes, and with airports remaining closed, no one was coming in and hotel occupancy dropped off the scale. Several large well-known Bangkok hotels reported the number of their let rooms being in single figures; I saw one reporting four rooms being let out of some 400. All this was taking place at the time of year when tourism is normally at its height just before Christmas and the New Year. The English language *Bangkok Post* reported simply, "… this year there is no high season", and estimates of the financial loss quickly left numbers behind and the most used words were "catastrophic" and "incalculable". Resultant unemployment was predicted in millions. Such a closure was not just unusual but unprecedented, indeed it was probably unique anywhere in the world. Despite its shooting-yourself-in-the-foot impact, the protesters were acquiescent about it all; one middle age lady protester I spoke to about its effects later said simply, "It had to be done".

The effects were still being felt months on and continued throughout the following year. The effect was not just on big companies but on individuals. I think the saddest thing I saw, a little time after the airport was re-opened, was a letter in a newspaper from a tourist who had been touring the north of the country. They had had a wonderful time, and they praised their guide, who had made their trip memorable, but they then said that when they met her she had bookings for every day through the peak season to the end of March; enough work to see her through the leaner times of year. When they left everything was cancelled – her diary contained not one single booking. One wonders how such people – she was a freelance – survived. I hope they gave her a big tip.

Eventually, the protesters went home and the airport re-opened. Dire predictions had been made about physical damage to the terminal building and equipment and about how long it might take to get things running again, but another unusual and characteristic aspect of this affair was that, having agreed to leave, the demonstrators formed work parties: litter was cleared, floors swept, all the paraphernalia of the occupation removed and no damage was found as airport workers returned to duty. As the government had caved in and agreed to many of their demands, protesters were presumably able to indulge in a smile or two as they went about this clear up. Airport operations resumed promptly, the greatest delays then being caused by aircraft having been stranded in the wrong place and having to be relocated to fit schedules.

So, the yellow-shirted protesters may have ultimately been smiling, but how did the travellers fare?

Well, despite the peculiar nature of the protest, the airport was firmly closed and tens of thousands of people were inconvenienced, some in a major way. Some people were stranded for a week or more and ran out of money (though a little government funding was arranged for hotel costs towards the end of the closure). A few people were not fazed: some British students I spoke to said simply, "no problem – back to the beach". But there was real heartbreak too: people missed weddings, job interviews and the hundred and one things that they had to return to. Lives changed. As with any such adverse situation, people in hotels, travel agents and elsewhere talked to each other. Transport sharing was arranged, friendships formed and, for all I know, relationships were started and babies were conceived. There was plenty of time for such things to occur, after all. Many people left by travelling to neighbouring countries, for instance Malaysia or Vietnam, and flying home from there. Bearing in mind that a train from Bangkok to Kuala Lumpur takes three days, such disruption was very real and often costly.

There was a plethora of ways in which people were affected. Just as the airport closed, I was in Singapore on business and due to meet my wife, who was scheduled to travel out from the United Kingdom, in Bangkok for some holiday. My flight back to Bangkok was cancelled, but at least, credit where credit is due, budget airline Air Asia on which I had flown from Bangkok to Singapore, made a swift

Chapter Seven

refund – but no other help available. "Must wait," I was told bluntly. I did not want my wife arriving in Bangkok, expecting me to meet her and whisk her off to the beach, to find me not even in the same country, so some serious research as to how I might proceed was called for. Meantime there remained the question of how – if – she would get into the country; more of this anon.

I spoke to a travel agent, to several local contacts in Singapore and emailed a couple of friends in Thailand. The top tip was always the same: fly to the holiday island of Phuket and travel into Bangkok by road. It sounded possible, though it was unlikely that I would be the only one trying to do just that. I had also telephoned my travel insurers, arranged through the bank Nat West. They took three quarters of an hour, two transfers and, I think, four people to tell me that they had no idea how this was to be dealt with and that I should phone again the next day. Just as urgent action was clearly called for as things got worse, they insisted on delay; another situation of a bank failing to recognise customer needs – thanks for nothing.

The day after I was due to fly – having spoken to the insurance company again only to be told that, having brooded about it for 24 hours, they had decided they couldn't help; they muttered darkly about terrorism, which did not seem to me a true description of events, so thanks for nothing again – I packed, went to the airport and arrived there just before 6 a.m. Now Singapore's airport is simply a marvel. It is modern, efficient – it just works and works well. When my budget airline had delivered me in just a few days earlier it had taken less than 15 minutes from the wheels of the plane touching the ground to my stepping into a taxi outside the terminal. Yes, really. The doors opened as the plane stopped, passport control was not far away, there were no queues and my suitcase was just coming onto the carousel as I approached it. A delegation should be sent from London's infamous Heathrow at once to study it – efficiency is possible. But if flights are all full – and they were – then even such an efficient set up as this finds it difficult to help.

I had discovered that three airlines had flights to Phuket that day. All three departed from different terminals. I made a circuit, walking corridors, waiting for shuttle buses and getting pretty hot in the process, only to have confirmed that everything was fully booked. But I could be waitlisted: that is put on a list of people who were essentially first reserve if anyone who had a firm booking failed to appear. This seemed worthwhile with only one of the airlines, the one with four flights scheduled through the day. Being waitlisted sounds good, but I found that one can only be waitlisted for one flight at a time, if you fail to get on, then the whole process starts again and, in the meantime, numbers of people may have been listed in front of you for the next one. After failing to get on two flights, but having made a point of talking to the same person each time I reapplied, I took his advice and listed myself not for the next flight, but for the last one of the day. I also discovered that the way this works is not just a matter of the order in which people are listed, rather it was described, somewhat mysteriously, as being dependent on, "… a number of factors".

I immediately asked what factors were involved, intent on trying to make sure that I somehow fitted the criteria. The shutters came down. Not a single hint as to how it worked was forthcoming. I tried to persist, but my informant was first vague, "Well, there are different, well factors. It is complicated". Maybe, but this was not helping me. Then he was adamant, "I really can't say more". It appeared that whatever these "factors" were, they were a deeply protected secret within the trade, a bit like who gets seats in the front row or upgraded to Business Class.

Nevertheless, some at least of these factors must have been on my side as I was the last passenger confirmed on the last flight of the day; after some 12 hours at the airport I was on my way. The 12 hours, it should be said, were neither a pleasant nor a comfortable time. It is obvious, when you think about it, I suppose, but the check-in area is for, well, for checking in, and it's a process that normally only lasts a few minutes. All the airport's comforts and delights are located after you leave this area and go through to the departure lounge. Here the only seats were hard shells, there was nowhere to sit and plug in a computer (well, Starbucks provided one place but that was monopolised throughout the whole day by the same group of young people) and the only comfort was yet another expensive drink in one of the cafés. It was tedious, too: conversations were possible, there were plenty of people held up and struggling to make some rescue arrangement just as I was, but most often both parties were guarded. The situation meant that other people had come to be regarded as competition; that if someone else got on a flight then you well might not. As many suspicious looks as smiles and pleasantries were exchanged.

So the hours dragged by. I read an entire book, but kept checking with the various desks too, and with the various televisions around that showed the news. Had anything changed? Was any new, better or easier option presenting itself? Had the airport in Bangkok reopened? So finally, after the long wait, an hour's flight seemed like nothing at all. I was on my way and I soon found myself in Phuket's airport, which was, no great surprise, overflowing with people. Here some small sign of organisation was in evidence. I was quickly directed upstairs to the departures lounge where, at a small table, tickets – well little scraps of paper with a number written on them in pencil for the organisation was pretty rudimentary – were available for coaches to Bangkok. At a cost of *baht* 800, this bit of my journey seemed like a bargain and a breeze. Numbers of coaches waited just outside the door, the next scheduled to leave in less than an hour. I bought some supplies and took my seat half an hour ahead of departure, as the coach slowly filled up both with regular travellers and others, like myself, who were on an emergency route.

The downside of all this was that the journey was 12 hours long and was to deposit passengers at a bus terminal demanding a further journey by taxi of maybe up to an hour to get into central Bangkok. Never mind, I was getting there. Although two stops were planned en route, I planned to sleep as much as possible during the journey; arrival was estimated at around 7 a.m. The passengers were a complete mixture: locals, visitors, young, old and with some in various degrees of desperation to reach the end of their journey. In the seat next to me I had a Frenchman, about 40 years old. He looked sober and quiet and apparently spoke very little English. After a while he went to sleep, as did I. Then his mobile phone rang... and rang. Finally, he found and answered it and engaged in a long conversation in French with someone who was probably on the other side of the world. This happened at least a dozen times. I caught the eye of a Thai man sitting alongside the Frenchman on the other side of the aisle. He smiled. But it seemed to be a sad "madness, but what can you do" sort of smile.

Perhaps this spurred me on, others were as annoyed as I was, so I moved from saying, "It would be nice if you could switch your phone off" to "Listen, you selfish idiot, for heaven's sake switch off your damn phone – it's the middle of the night and people are trying to sleep". The latter got sounds of general agreement from passengers sitting round about, and was apparently understood because finally he did turn it off. That done, we promptly stopped at a service station, waking everyone again. Throughout the stop the Frenchman prowled up and down alongside the coach, phone firmly to ear; the fate of something important clearly dependent on this communication – maybe he worked for an airline and was busy sorting out just our sort of problem. Back on board I slept fitfully. Every time I stirred the coach seemed to be in the middle of overtaking something on a narrow bit of the road and just making it as headlights, and sometimes a horn, loomed coming the other way.

As daylight returned, the coach was well into the city and just after 7 a.m. we arrived safely at the coach station pretty much as planned. The station was a dusty concrete desert with a couple of buildings and a few other coaches parked up, but few signs of life. Passengers disembarked and a couple of staff at the station came forward to get luggage out of the compartment where it was stored under the bus. People watched for their cases and many cast an eye in the other direction to where just two or three taxis waited. I managed to grab my suitcase and a taxi and, after a journey through city streets already awake and busy, checked into my hotel just after 8 a.m. The usual smiling welcome seemed muted and at check-in there were mystified looks as I announced my name. "Aren't you expecting me?" I asked. This got a smile. "Oh yes, have booking, but we did not expect you to get here – welcome!" New arrivals were currently few and far between. I unpacked and treated myself to a good breakfast and then hastened to check my email. While I had spent a total of almost 30 hours getting to Bangkok from Singapore, what had been happening to my wife?

Bangkok airport was still closed. Normally it has between four and 600 flights arriving every day. At this stage, arrangements had been made to get a few flights into Bangkok; all the talk had evidently led to something. But only about 40 or 50 flights were making it – landing at an ex-military airport near the resort of Pattaya, normally used in a minimal way for a few charter flights. My email told me that my wife was due to arrive there. How, I wondered. I later discovered that with her London flight cancelled she had spent a day dialling the airline office only to find it permanently engaged; no surprise there. With two flights a day normally going to Bangkok that meant there must have been thousands of people wanting information. The following morning – a Saturday – she got a train to London and went to Thai Airway's office in London's West End. The "shop-front" office was closed, but lights were on upstairs and she knew people were manning the telephones (though when she had dialled repeatedly from the train she had continued to get nothing but an engaged tone).

She knocked on the door. No response. She knocked harder and for longer... and longer.

Chapter Seven

Eventually someone came to the door, no doubt lengthening the queue waiting on the telephone just a little more. They listened to her tale of woe and within half an hour she left, having been moved to a confirmed flight from Frankfurt to Bangkok's emergency airport leaving the following morning. Despite the short notice, a little time on the internet secured her a London to Frankfurt flight and she too was on her way. Her flight out of Frankfurt was held up on departure and arrived in Bangkok two hours late and simultaneously with a flight from Mumbai. The combined number of arriving passengers totally overwhelmed the minimal ad hoc facilities at the emergency airport. The one rudimentary luggage carousel was besieged. The younger passengers from the Indian flight pushed forward and suitcases were hoisted high and passed back over peoples' heads. Gradually the crowd cleared; nevertheless it took six hours from landing to her meeting with me in central Bangkok. She had given up on a coach being provided and clubbed together with a group of other passengers to hire a minibus. Finally she walked into the hotel where I was waiting and we enjoyed a, slightly tearful, reunion. I had arranged transport to our holiday resort in Hua Hin, indeed the driver had arrived a little time before and then slept soundly in a corner of Reception until my wife caught up and we were ready to leave.

After all this we had a smooth and uneventful drive to the coast and finally arrived in Hua Hin just 24 hours later than our planned arrival date; a minor miracle in the circumstances, a fact confirmed on arrival by the amazement and smiles our being there created at check-in. Certainly, if my wife had not taken the action she did in London – an initiative, I have to say, that impressed me mightily – the holiday would have been ruined. No flights went from London to Bangkok during the following eight or nine days. I am not sure what I would have done, particularly bearing in mind that at the time it permanently looked as if the airport would reopen any minute. With no knowledge of what would happen, we would both have spent a frustrating time checking events day by day. The holiday would have been stillborn.

At the earliest possible moment, we sat down looking out over the sea, ordered a cold drink and compared notes, congratulating ourselves on both our respective action and the luck that no doubt contributed to our success. During our holiday we kept half an eye on the airport situation as it continued, and continued, hoping it would be over before we were due to go home; it made a rather bizarre background to a relaxing time. To begin with the town was full of people trying to leave, and later this situation was replaced by a general emptiness because few new people were arriving. Ordinary Thais appeared embarrassed by the whole thing and largely at a loss as to what to say about it, so naturally they smiled. At every stage people seemed to believe that it could not possibly last longer and there were several false rumours about re-opening before normality finally did return and it was smiles all round.

As for many people, the personal legacy to all this was, in part, the cost. We succeeded in bypassing the airport problem and we had a great holiday, but it did cost more than expected. Not least, we had both had to buy an additional air ticket for part of our journeys and, as I mentioned, my first contact with my insurance company had proved... well, let's say it was less than helpful. So, once we were back home and despite their previous attitude, I contacted them again asking for a claim form. Even providing basic details on the telephone brought a put-off and again a mention of the word "terrorism" seemed clearly designed to make me forget the whole thing. I did not. I was there. The protest may have been many things: surprising, large, unprecedented, annoying, inconvenient, but terrorism it was not. I persevered and, despite receiving other similar comments dismissing the possibility of a successful payment out of hand, I submitted a written claim and the necessary receipts.

Time passed and eventually a letter came rejecting the claim. It was very vague about why this conclusion had been reached, essentially saying that my circumstances were not covered, so I telephoned again. Further discussion about the nature of the airport closure followed, none encouraging, but it was mentioned that I could opt to have the matter "reassessed". They asked if I wanted that, in a tone that implied strongly that it would be a waste of time. But I did want it reassessed. I wrote confirming that this should be done, and waited. The result was only another letter and another rejection.

My contacts continued, both with the bank through which my insurance was handled and direct with the insurance company. The bank seemed to want only to keep right out of it, suggesting that rather than their taking an interest in the way their chosen insurer handled their customers I should pursue matters through the Financial Ombudsman Service. Weird, when what I wanted was their support in dealing with the insurer. Surely they wanted their customers well and fairly dealt with and happy? Apparently not; maybe they had other things on their mind. Come to think of it, they must have had other things on their mind at a time when banks were in deep trouble worldwide, but it would have been nice if they had made some attempt to help.

I wrote again at some length, describing the nature of the protest that had closed the airport and commenting point by point on why I felt that this was in no way covered by their quoted "not-a-chance-in-hell" clause, which went on about war, hostilities and right through to virtually the invasion of marauding foreign hordes intent on rape and pillage. They contested this, but only in an overall sense; no attempt was made to explain exactly why they thought I was wrong and they were right or precisely which part of the clause they considered applied. Their letters were inclined to the ambiguous and replete with a business gobbledegook that made it somewhat difficult to follow what was happening, if anything was actually happening. I imagined them just playing a waiting game – *Wait a couple more weeks, write again, say something vague and see if that makes him go away.*

They began to split the issues, saying for instance that my wife's costs were excluded for some other reason than mine, then later after I had queried this they said immediately that that was an error. They also kept asking for more information and receipts – including some already requested and that I had sent previously – questions that could (should?) surely have been asked for early on in the process.

Then, four months on and without explanation, a cheque arrived; two cheques, actually, as they again separated different issues, my costs, my wife's and so on. I was of course delighted. It had been a tedious battle and a handful of minor costs remained omitted – wrongly, I thought. For instance, although they accepted that I had gone to Bangkok by way of

Chapter Seven

Phuket, and paid me the cost of the Singapore to Phuket airfare, they refused to pay the coach fare from Phuket to the city because the only receipt available on boarding the coach was a scrap of paper with the number "8" written on it in pencil. What did they think I'd done on getting to Phuket? Walked? Hopped in the Tardis and appeared instantly outside my hotel? I rather wished I'd got a taxi, which would have cost at least ten times as much but provided a receipt. Nevertheless, by persevering I had succeeded in getting paid for the vast majority of my extra costs.

The whole claim process still left a bad taste in my mouth. I suspect many people would have given up at an earlier stage; indeed, the handling of the claim seemed designed specifically to put one off and encourage this. If that's true, then this was a tactic that seems to me plain dishonest, but which could doubtless save the insurance companies a lot of money as many thousands of people were in trouble because of the airport closure.

What's the moral here? In any such disputes it apparently pays to assume that you are being put off and, when you believe right is on your side, to pursue the logic of the matter repeatedly and resolutely for longer than you want. In this case, my doing so took the best part of four months. Maybe I should write again asking for interest to be paid for the time they took to pay up. Wait a minute, silly me, with the interests rates the banks are paying at present that would be a real waste of time.

Having received payment I wrote again to the bank about their chosen insurer in a way that I felt was helpful and constructive in terms of future service. Their reply remained mealy-mouthed: it was terrorism they said. The payment had been a "goodwill gesture". I should feel free to go to the Financial Ombudsman Service. They said that they were "sorry that you needed to contact us" and were "grateful to you for bringing this to our attention", yet – it seemed to me – they could just not wait to forget the whole thing. I wondered about demanding that the matter was reviewed at a more senior level, but I did not. The whole thing had already been ridiculously time consuming – besides I'm sure that their senior bankers would be far too busy spending their large bonuses to give any attention to me. I banked the cheques and moved on.

It made me think of a story told of the famous actress, Edith Evans. Offended by a fellow actress, she did not not speak to her friend for some years. Finally another actor told her that surely this had gone on long enough, suggesting that she "forgive and forget". She protested, but finally agreed to end the silence and re-established contact; though she said that she would forgive… she would, she said, never forget. Well said. For me the name Nat West will always prompt thoughts of evasion and inefficiency.

The holiday was saved, though (well, with just one day lost), and given the large numbers of visitors that had not got through, the service and the smiles doled out to those of us who were there were exceptional.

Chapter Seven

Chapter Eight

FRIEND INDEED

Books and friends should be few but good.
Traditional proverb

Distance may not make maintaining a friendship easy, but it is certainly a factor that defines a good one and the ability to meet with people you see rarely and pick up with them as if you had spoken on the day before is a rare and valuable thing. When geography divides you it used to make for a more difficult process, with long gaps punctuated by the occasional postcard or Christmas round robin note. Now, of course, email and a profusion of other technological wizardry from Skype to webcams helps the process of keeping long distance friendships fresh.

But they have to start somewhere. Some years back, we picked a resort in Thailand out of a brochure and stayed at Hua Hin on Thailand's Gulf of Thailand coast over New Year. It was very good too and the New Year's Eve bash was quite an extravaganza: music and entertainment, including a wonderful Chinese dragon wending its way through the tables set out in the gardens that abutted the beach, and fireworks to see in the New Year. Over a few days it was apparent that some people always disappeared along the beach in the evening to where a small hotel also sat right on the beach. Exploring, we found a tiny hotel with an eating area in the garden, prices a fraction of those in the resort and excellent food. Eating there regularly we got talking to other people, including those staying there who praised it highly. By the time the holiday was ending we had decided to return to Hua Hin the following year, got a brochure about the tiny hotel, which had only a dozen rooms, and made a booking there and then.

One lady was much in evidence: she gave us the brochure we asked for, she supervised the cooking, she did some of the serving at table and, as we discovered later, as owner she did pretty much everything else too. When she was in the kitchen she wore a strange truncated chef's white hat and her diminutive but energetic figure was always in evidence and always busy. When we returned the next year she welcomed us effusively and both we and another couple we had met up with last time and who had also returned began to get to know her better. The small hotel had been bought as an investment, but she loved running it and found she was good at doing so too. We met her husband and two teenage sons, who spent most of their time in Bangkok but visited the hotel regularly. Siripan not only made our holiday memorable but, as we returned regularly each year, which we did along with our friends, over some 10 years became a real friend.

Much more than just being a guest in her hotel began to be involved. She would join us for dinner so that we could chat, and sometimes, when dinner was ordered from one of her young waitresses they would return from the kitchen saying, "Cannot order, food cooking now, Siripan coming soon". After a little while she would appear, flanked by her two waitresses, all carrying steaming dishes. A spread of food would be laid out and everyone would tuck in; there was always a mixture, and my not liking the spiciest of food was always remembered. It might sound a bit dictatorial: you try to order a meal and something else appears instead – no discussion. But it was all good, we did not complain and we loved her joining us. Such meals were charged at a ridiculously low rate, just so much per head rather than slavishly linking to the actual dishes served. Indeed, in more than 10 years of staying at the hotel, a bill was never signed, yet the total at the end of your stay was always accurately recorded and spot on.

Sometimes we also went out with her to eat elsewhere. A favourite place was on the pier at nearby Cha Am, a fishing village in an area now swelled by hotels and other establishments catering for tourists. These outings involved a driver (it was about 20 minutes away) who, on arrival at Cha Am's coastal road, would wind his way further and further into the depths of the market area. Any suggestion that a particular establishment looked good and might be worth a try was always greeted by Siripan in the same way: "Not good, only for tourists".

At the one she favoured we saw few, if any, tourists. A wide, concrete, canvass-covered area, spread with simple plastic chairs and tables, was no luxury restaurant, though it looked out across the water where fishing boats came and went. But the food was superb. Mostly it was fish and mostly, too, you chose what you wanted from what was swimming in tanks set around the entrance. Tasty. *A-roi*, as the Thais say: delicious. With a local guide to pick what was best, it was a real treat. She has organised many an outing: the elephant reserve described in Chapter 2 was but one of her "surprises".

Chapter Eight

Because she knows the areas well, her outings often involve shortcuts. One such trip saw her little Mazda bogged down in mud along a rain-sodden track. In a moment she had succeeded in getting a small group of men working in the field alongside to abandon their work for long enough to push us out and get us to firm ground again. The rescue caused much smiling and merriment. It is another aspect of the attitude to time in Thailand that people will take time in such circumstances to lend a hand.

Because we always visited at the start of the year, the highlight of these stays at Siripan's hotel was New Year's Eve. In a Buddhist country Christmas is no big deal, though shops of course relate to the season, and New Year is seen as a more important holiday as is the Thais' own New Year which is in April. In such a tiny establishment it was not possible to outdo the big resorts, where incidentally their New Year's evening's do become both compulsory and very expensive over the years, but she was determined to make it special for her guests, and she did. Because many guests were regulars and because of the way she did things, everything was very informal. She put on a special evening of food and entertainment. I am sure it must have been long in the planning and there was always ample evidence of the thought that went into it but, on the day, things appeared to start only in the early afternoon. Hotel guests were organised to help set out the necessary tables, both to sit at and for food to be served from, in the garden overlooking the beach together with the accompanying chairs. I say organised, regular guests were ordered to appear at a set hour and others were encouraged to join in and help if they wished.

Always there were some things set up that were unexplained. Enquiry produced only a repeated, "Later, later". And later all became clear with, for instance, a pile of unexplained sacks forming an ad hoc plinth for an ice sculpture. A man-high block of ice delivered as the evening started was gradually carved into a mythical winged creature that shone in the lights. As the final blow was struck on the ice, the skilful sculptor, who seemed absurdly young, grinned broadly and took a bow as guests applauded. Somehow the statue lasted long into the evening despite the heat.

The evening, a long, friendly, informal affair, consisted of an extensive many-coursed buffet set out under the trees which were all festooned with seasonal lights. There was always some sort of entertainment laid on, maybe around ten in the evening, which finished with fireworks on the stroke of midnight. Amazingly, Thai time at that moment always seemed to relate accurately to the rest of the world. Modest fireworks perhaps, compared with the big resorts, but set right there on the beach in front of the garden. In a tiny hotel the entertainment had to be simple, there was no huge budget to be spent. One year I remember she organised a group of children from the local primary school who sang and danced for us. It was a delight and it was difficult to tell who enjoyed it most, the guests or the children. One guest had a banjo and, after the performance, played for the children and taught them songs like the Burl Ives number "The Ugly Bug Ball". This was a serendipitous thing. In a comparatively small group, even with friends and visitors too, there were only perhaps 40 people there; to have someone with a suitable instrument and a real ability to sing was a bonus. And the banjo suited what he did; the kids loved it

Chapter Eight

and were soon singing along. It could have been a less suitable instrument or something awful, which reminds me of the old saying that the definition of a gentleman is a man who can play the accordion – but doesn't.

Another thing I loved and which sticks in my mind is the notice that always went up on the day of the event. On a large white board, inscribed in various colours, Siripan listed the timings planned for the evening: drinks, food, entertainment and so on. But it always ended the same way:

Midnight: Happy New Year – fireworks.

Then… the instruction:

Everyone go to bed! And no early breakfast!

It says a good deal about the event, the guests and of course Siripan herself that this last instruction caused no offence – indeed we loved it. Many guests at the small hotel were regulars and many became friends: in my case I have spent New Year in Thailand every year for more than 20 years with friends first met there. Siripan gave those gatherings something of the quality of a small house party rather than the formality of a hotel event and they were all the better for it.

By breakfast time the following morning, her small group of staff had cleared everything away and, provided you did not buck the system and try to get breakfast too early, then everything was back to normal. For some years annual visits to this charming small hotel were a highlight of my year, I was not the only one that came to count this equally charming lady and her family as special friends. Sadly, some years on, divorce meant that the hotel, which she owned with her husband, had to be sold and we and others had to find another hotel if we wanted to continue our New Year visits as we felt that the old place would never be the same without her (and it wasn't, which is why I am not recommending it and quoting its name). It was, no surprise here, Siripan who introduced us to another small hotel nearby and that has since proved a worthy successor.

Now this is a competent and talented lady who had run a hotel, albeit a small one, for some years. She had organised staff, marketing, bookings and the whole important area of meals, menus and all that goes with that. It added up to a full time job, more than full time in high season, and in doing it she had turned her hand successfully to many things. With the hotel sold, and her sons grown up, she was not going to retire and relax at home. Well, actually, she first needed a new home. She could have rented or bought, indeed she did rent for a while, but she also designed and built a new house for herself in a quiet spot a little to the back of the town.

Building in Thailand is not quite like it is in the west. We visited when the house was up but unfinished. The tiling was being done in the kitchen, two bathrooms and every floor in the house including the stairs. Doing this involved the best part of 20 skilled workers, all women. They did not seem to get in each other's way, did an excellent job and it was finished in two and a half days. Compare this with organising one reliable tradesperson in England and you may despair.

Since then, Siripan has poured her organising talents and mafia-like connections into a series of projects. She has renovated and let residential property, renovated an old building, actually ruin would be a better description, into a beautiful small guest house, run it for a while and sold it on, started and established a coffee shop, and bought and sold land. Not content with that, as I write she is currently

Chapter Eight

turning into a virtual civil engineer, designing and creating a small complex of streams and lakes alongside a piece of land out in the country on which she intends to build a small number of houses. She has named this place *Baan Naab Doa*, which means "Counting Stars House", and sent me an email saying: "… at night if you are sitting out door you will see lot of stars up to the sky so we are counting them… one by one… it might be so romantic at night time, hope not any elephant step on me in the dark."

Even though only some 3000 stars are visible to the naked eye at one time, the night sky in such a place is awesome. With virtually no lights in evidence on the ground, the sky seems awash with stars and one can imagine what impact such a sight must have had in historical times, when just what it implied was hardly known. Her philosophy with this project is that the place must be made beautiful before any building starts. She is not just laying this down on an already beautiful site – it is near to town, but isolated with a 360 degree view to mountains a little different in each direction – rather, she is enhancing the already entrancing natural features.

The guest house is an example of her attitude and approach. The place, a pair of semi-detached houses, was utterly dilapidated and abandoned. It was owned by a bank which had taken it to pay a debt and then just left it to rot. Trees grew out of the floor and electric wires dangled out of the ceiling. I remember saying to her, "You're mad, you will never convert it". Her reply was totally matter of fact. "Sure, no problem, will be done, will be beautiful". Not only did she organise and supervise the renovation work, she finished the place beautifully. Each bedroom was different: the colours, silk cushions and overall effect were a delight. Considerable time and effort was spent to create comparatively small effects: for instance, she created a small bridge over a pond at the door as "It is good luck to enter crossing water".

Good luck was not, I suspect, the reason this project was successful, it was surely more a question of hard work. Once finished, it quickly became a useful little business and made her a profit when she sold it on. Again, I will not mention the name as I am sure it cannot be so special now she is not at the helm. In between all this she has helped a long list of people with various less formal projects, finding homes for foreigners retiring to Thailand for instance, and continuing to be a caring mother to her two, now grown up, sons. She keeps in touch with a number of overseas friends like myself with regular emails, some informative, some touching and nearly all with a delightful touch of her wicked sense of humour. She speaks good English, but this does tend to go just a touch wobbly in writing and this adds to the fun.

Siripan is the sort of person, perhaps something of a rarity, who you count yourself lucky to have as a friend because she is not only a pleasure to know but adds something special to your life. What is more, she also, way back, was one cause of my meeting a couple who have become very special friends and who I mentioned as joining my wife and I on many a wonderful holiday. Holidaying with friends can be a disaster, and there are friends, even good friends, with whom it should be avoided perhaps at all costs, but Jack and Silvia are the other extreme and we find that their company makes any holiday special. Together we have got great pleasure from our many visits to Thailand.

Visiting a country, especially a number of times, begins to give you a perspective on the place. Really getting to know people there casts much more light. Siripan has been a powerful influence on my love of Thailand developing, and a variety of incidents have taken place over the years to make this so. When one of her sons, Pub, took the traditional Thai route of becoming a monk, for a period of about six months as I remember, she took us to visit him at the temple. He met us wearing saffron robes, his head shaven, and took us around the site where he was spending time, some quiet time in contemplation, some hard work. An early rise each day saw him and his fellow monks walking out to find breakfast, or indeed food for the day, donated by well-wishers around the area. Monks must collect all their food in this way and eat only two meals each day. Despite the tough routine, he was in good heart and took some pride in showing us around. At this stage he had completed his education, including a spell at a language school in Britain he attended with his brother. I am not sure how much about student life in England he relayed back to his mother, but I met them a couple of times on their visit and they seemed to be enjoying it. Certainly Pub has done well, joining an international hotel group and working his way up. He now lives and works in Phuket.

*

On one occasion we met with Pub, pronounced "pup" in the contrary way of Thai words, in Phuket. He is on the management team of the excellent Renaissance Hotel in the north of Phuket and we had emailed him to see if he would like to have dinner. He came on the first day and left saying we must meet again and that he would "arrange something". A message then arrived saying we should be ready at midday on

Smile Because It Happened

Thursday. At noon, a minibus drew up at the Reception of our hotel and the driver met us at the entrance. He was dressed in a denim jacket, shaggy hair spilling out of a black baseball cap, and looked as if he rode a Harley Davidson and played jazz saxophone in the evening. Toon, as he proved to be called, peered through steel spectacles and handed us a large envelope. Inside there was a typed itinerary showing what we should see, where we should stop for refreshments, with menu recommendations included – "here you should try the curried crab with noodles" – where the best shops were (the central plaza proved to be huge and much more modern than I imagined) and, ultimately, where he would meet us for dinner.

Toon spoke little English but was a master of mime and sign language. He was also exceptionally solicitous, shepherding us in and out of the bus and heading us off in the right direction when, for instance, we walked through the old town. This is an area of quaint traditional shop-houses, small shops below and living accommodation above, many of them 200 years old. Here, too, are various notable buildings, including the first neighbourhood bank in Thailand; the On On Hotel, the first hotel in Phuket; and the China Inn faced with double lacquered doors and built more than 100 years ago. There are a plethora of styles reflected here: Chinese, Portuguese and art deco mix with more modern innovations. It's an interesting area in which to wander and perhaps to shop or eat.

We had an excellent tour. At lunchtime we ate in a fabulous Thai restaurant, "D Phuket": it's simple, but the food and service are excellent. The owner, *Khun* Panaret, who spoke excellent English and started by saying "Call me Penny", was seemingly pleased to chat. She had a home in

Chapter Eight

Hua Hin, from which we had just arrived, and we compared notes about the growth of the town over the years. After we had eaten, she arranged an additional visit to a cashew nut emporium. These are a Phuket speciality and here the juice, which comes from the fruit of the tree not the nut, is also regarded as a delicacy both to drink and to use in cooking. We had a demonstration of the preparation and a tasting of nuts blended with everything from coffee to sesame seeds to make tasty snacks. Though it might be said that they are prejudiced, Methee, the business in question, set out almost magical qualities for their juice. It is full of vitamins, natural fibres and antioxidants "proven five times of orange". Drinking it evidently, and I quote, benefits you thus: "Refresh and energize, quench thirst and relieve sore throat, relief from symptoms of ordinary flue, improves excretory functions, relief from constipation, enhances eyesight, skin, nerves and bones, prevents gastric ulcer and anaemia, enhance immunization." Wow! Empty the medicine cabinet and fill the larder.

*

Siripan loves cooking; indeed, much of the time I have spent with her has been around a table. Something that makes many people smile in Thailand is the food, well not just the food but the whole experience of eating. I love it. Actually I do not love it all and one of the few Thai phrases that I have mastered is *mai pet* which means food that is not too spicy. Thai spiciness can catch you out. I once chose a minced beef dish at a small restaurant, indeed was recommended it by a friend, and I found it very good as I ate it. But after about 10 minutes my mouth went completely numb. The whole of the bottom half of my face felt like I had been to the dentist on the kind of visit which demands liberal use of anaesthetic; the sort that involves wearing a bib, a sure sign that there is going to be blood, and a needle as long and threatening as a light sabre. The numbness lasted a couple of hours during which time I was only able to mumble incoherently and mentally deleted the beef dish from my list of dishes to order again.

One of Siripan's ambitions has long been to write a cookbook. This was always a vague thought rather than a firm plan, and she knew that, like Winnie the Pooh's spelling, her written English was a bit wobbly. With part of my income coming from being a "writer for hire", I try to visit the London Book Fair regularly. It is usually held in London's Olympia and is a huge event, most important to publishers for meeting the many foreign visitors who are seeking the translation rights that form one element of their income. But my visiting it is a useful way to check out the circumstances of the industry and meet people who might want to hire a humble hack.

I found myself chatting to the two principles of a small publisher who had published books of mine in the past; *nothing* I suggested created any interest at all. Finally, almost as I moved on, I asked "What kind of thing *are* you looking to add to your list?". The answer was cookbooks and I quickly enquired about a Thai one. A deal was soon set up and Siripan was in receipt of a contract. My role? To smooth out her English a little. Emails began to fly to and fro across the world about this and I began to try to clarify what she was saying. Did 3/4 mean three quarters or between three

Chapter Eight

and four? Is a Thai tablespoon (tbsp) the same as a European one and just how thin did "cut thin" imply?

Gradually a manuscript came together. The relevant number of recipes was no problem, though if I am honest my part took a good deal longer that I had thought. The whole thing amazed my family and friends: that I, well known to know nothing of cooking and struggling to produce tea and un-burnt toast at the same time, should have anything, even the tiniest little thing, to do with a cookbook, was wholly and completely ridiculous. I had no input to the content, I hasten to add, and the book, which focuses on easy to prepare dishes and is the only Thai cookbook published in the U.K. actually written by a Thai, is now available (*Everyday Thai Cookery*, Siripan Akvanich, published by Spring Hill). I know how good her cooking and her recipes are so it deserves to do well.

Knowing someone like Siripan has helped bring Thailand to life. She is also an inspiration. She has achieved so much, yet seems to tackle everything in such a matter of fact way. If anything needs to be obtained or done she knows just the right person to do it, whether it is organising just which fisherman will deliver fish to the hotel door early each morning – "Must be the best" – to working out just where the culvert should go on her country land and organising a mechanical digger to sort it out; nothing nonplusses her. Despite her charm, she can be tough too. I have seen her see off troublemakers from her hotel restaurant, the local equivalent of lager louts, and once going into whirlwind mode when my wife had a day or two in hospital locally with a bad back.

Siripan was evidently appalled at how she was being treated. In moments she had staff running round: the care arrangements were changed, the nurses' rota was changed, the menu was changed and, though the remonstrating was done in Thai, it was pretty clear from the faces around that she commanded serious respect.

That said, I have great respect for the medical services in Thailand. It is normally both efficient and pragmatic. On one occasion I woke in my hotel to find my chest covered in spots. I thought I should check it out. The doctor, summoned promptly by my hotel, arrived and looked at my chest. His English was good, his succinctness an object lesson in precision. "You have chicken pox," he pronounced confidently. It emerged later that I had been unknowingly exposed to a friend's children with the disease before I flew east. I asked whether there was something I could do, some medicine I could take. "No," he replied simply, adding, "Go home quickly: as an adult it will make you very ill". He smiled sympathetically. *Mai pen rai* had never been more appropriate. Still feeling okay, the spots being the only symptom, I paid his bill, telephoned the airline, got an earlier flight and flew home. He was right: once home, flu-like symptoms set in in a big way and I was in bed for more than a week.

In my wife's case, still worried that she might not be being fed properly, Siripan made apple pie to take to the evening visiting hours. To my amazement, she got me sitting in her car, muttering "This is crazy", with a plate of apple pie and ice cream on my knee. Even in Thailand's heat she managed to get us to the hospital, find a parking space, reach the ward and deliver it before the ice cream melted. She is quite a character; I am inclined to think that "charming" fails to cover it; I am also pretty sure that she must have magic powers. Long may we be able to keep in touch.

Chapter Eight

Chapter Nine

AMONGST THE RUINS

Here, where the world is quiet.
Algernon Charles Swinbune

Normally Bangkok's airport is not closed. It is host to thousands of flights every week, and sees them through with efficiency and thoroughness. Indeed, the most stringent security operates. On one departure I walked through the x-ray arch and made it buzz. I was waved over with a wand and the source was identified as two small *baht* coins in my trouser pocket. I thought that would be the end of the matter, but I had to put the coins on a tray so that they could be passed through the machine handling luggage and individually x-rayed. They evidently proved to be no more than simple coins and so I was allowed to join my flight; now that's thorough.

Most of the flights here use modern jets, though not all. In another attempt to explore this country, I made a trip some way north of Bangkok to Sukhothai. This is an ancient, now ruined city: a world renowned and beautiful place, it is now a designated an international Heritage Site. Starting this excursion, it somehow seemed incongruous to walk out of Bangkok's massive and modern airport terminal towards a small plane with two engines driving propellers and with a capacity of well less than a hundred passengers. As passengers left the terminal, the plane in front of us looked

Chapter Nine

like a toy, something a six-year old would want to whiz around the room making rrrrring noises.

Having climbed the steps to the plane, which appeared to be made out of the same material as an airline meal tray, I said to the flight attendant, "Isn't this a bit small?" She immediately went into extreme "reassure-passenger" mode and told me it would be fine, it was reliable, it was in use every day and that I would love it as there were only to be a couple of dozen passengers on board. "Plenty of space," she said with a broad, encouraging smile. Yes, and less people to be killed if it failed, I thought, though my question had not actually meant that its appearance worried me. It looked modern and anyway I don't dwell on the hazards of flying. It is, after all, supposed to be safer than crossing a busy road, though if this maxim was coined by a statistician who had experienced Bangkok's notorious traffic that is not so encouraging. Perhaps it was the same statistician who calculated that in today's mad world when a new danger of air travel is that there might be a bomb on the plane, the chances of there being *two* bombs on board is infinitesimal. So he always felt safer if he took one with him. Sorry, not really. Anyway, as I thought of all this it then occurred to me that if anything *did* go wrong with this small plane it would not be like a jumbo going down and prompting front page worldwide headlines saying "Horrific aircraft disaster kills 400"; there might only be a small item buried on page nine, saying: "Small aircraft missing, a few unimportant people unaccounted for". Fingers crossed then.

We took off on time and, an hour or so later, landed safely at Sukhothai after what proved to be a comfortable and uneventful flight. To say this airport was a touch smaller than the one at Bangkok is like saying that a gnat is a tad smaller than a jumbo jet. There was a runway, a taxi area and a tiny terminal that hardly justified the name: it was a small, covered, open-sided area into which luggage was unloaded from a pick-up truck. I have seen bigger garden sheds. Around about it was just countryside. An elderly Volvo sent by my hotel waited outside and sped me to the town in little more than half an hour.

The main street was a profusion of shops and businesses: motor cycle repair shops, pharmacies, restaurants and retailers of all sorts. Many shops flowed out onto the pavement, their wares displayed for every passer by to see and step around. Ruean Hotel was down a quiet, narrow side road and the car pulled into a high-walled courtyard surrounded on three sides with buildings each, with an attractive, sweeping Thai-style roof covered in dark red tiles. The car slowed as it entered the courtyard and stopped just short of two enormous white rabbits sitting contentedly munching greenery and right in the way. These were truly the brontosaurus of the rabbit world and seemed to me to be the size of decent-sized dogs. They clearly had strong territorial rights and stared at the car for a few moments with a how-dare-you kind of look, before lolloping very slowly out of the way to allow the car to run forward and stop in front of the reception area. I later discovered that they were pets of the owner's daughter. They seemed to have a good sense of self-preservation and never went near the road.

I checked in. The owner smiled, gave me a potted description of the treats in store around the area and I was shown to my room; one of just 20 or so, mine was at the far corner of the rooms ringing the swimming pool. By now it

Chapter Nine

was evening. I had a tour arranged for the morning, but for now planned to do little more than unpack and have dinner.

Let me give some advice to the hotels of Thailand, especially those located in more isolated situations: make sure that the televisions in your bedrooms are able to play DVDs. Why? Well, let's face it, for foreign visitors, especially those travelling alone, Thai television is hardly a profusion of must-see entertainment. There are a number of channels, yes, but if you don't speak Thai they are wholly mysterious. It is sometimes even difficult to work out what kind of programme is showing. I recognise the news, or a quiz programme, but there are many programmes that are difficult even to categorise: dramas seem to overlap with other genres and you see programmes where one moment chases and sword fights are in progress, the next romance is in the air followed swiftly by something that makes a studio audience laugh: all very odd. Later I asked about television at reception – "No DVD, cannot do" – but what do Thais like to watch? "We want to dream," I was told "Not like real life, best about rich people, love-no-love, jealousy, exciting and always funny. Yes, must be funny. Actors (*Phra ek* is leading man) must be handsome, girls sexy (*Nang ek* is the heroine) and we want *always* a happy ending.". So now I know. Mind you, you must wait to get all this. An hour long programme usually has so many advertisements in it that it takes an hour and a half to reach that happy ending.

More important to the visitor, programmes here just do not promise an evening of engaging entertainment. I have never observed a guest in a Thai hotel poring over the TV programme guide and looking up to say, "I must watch that", not even once. So, when you can play a DVD, doing so makes a nice diversion after dinner and before sleep. Hence the advice to hotel proprietors: this is a decision factor for some people in picking which hotel to stay in.

At Ruean, no DVDs could be played and the television was solely that; it did not even offer the dubious repetitive delights of the ubiquitous CNN. Lucky I had a good book. Indeed, my philosophy for packing, especially for a journey with long flights, hours in airports and other inevitably idle moments, is to pack the books first and then squeeze in the clothes for which space remains. I even arrange things so that I have a book easily accessible when faced with a long, slow immigration queue, and have occasionally looked up to find people overtaking me as the queue has moved forward and I am lost in my reading. The acquisition of a Kindle has recently made all this easier and I love it. Even so, the first time I used it overseas, having spent some time lovingly loading it with things I was just longing to read, it stopped working a few pages off the end of a great thriller. It was not the same reading the end some weeks later when I was home and Amazon replaced it. Annoying, and it has happened again since – twice – so I am on my fourth one; the wonders of modern technology are sometimes less than perfect. Perhaps some clandestine element of the publishing industry is sabotaging them so that we have to travel with some real books as back up. Anyway, I enjoyed a good dinner, sat comfortably with a good book and retired early, ready for an early departure in the morning.

*

Chapter Nine

The hotel had arranged a car and driver and we set off for the drive to the ancient city, a journey of only half an hour or so. Once out past the edge of the town, much of the road seemed to be almost continuous village. Houses, small shops and eating places lined the road, all very small scale and all busy with local people going about their lives. Apart from the Heritage site itself, this was not a tourist area and, apart from the occasional sign for an international brand like Coca Cola, I saw no signs in English. If we slowed, and it was the sort of road where this happened regularly for everything from a restaurant on a trolley crossing the road to untidy road works as a patch of tarmac damaged by heavy rain was slowly repaired, then often people waved and smiled. I am always struck by how the Thais seem to enjoy the fact that other people love their country. They seem to know they live somewhere special and it is taken for granted that others should find it interesting and enjoyable. You can wander alone in many places, guaranteed some smiles and conversations too, with those you pass if you want to pause on your way.

Once at the site, although it was hot and dusty, the place seemed cool compared with Bangkok, although perhaps this was an illusion as there was so much greenery: grass and trees all around created a feeling of parkland. In every direction there were signs of the old city. Terracotta-coloured ruins glinted through the trees and, as we followed one of the narrow, but well-kept roads that threaded their way through the park, the variety of shapes and structure became clear. I had seen a couple of coaches at one point, but people were evidently well spread out as there seemed hardly a person in sight. Once well into the Heritage site, I conferred with my driver. I had made a list of places to see. He deleted some – "Very small, nothing to see" – but added others – "Must see this". In due course I found that one of his additions was to prove to be the best spot of all.

We stopped first at *Wat* Mahathai (the temple of the great relic), a vast place, known locally, my guide told me, simply as *Wat* Yai (the large temple). This simple, if rather unimaginative, name reminded me of the only word I understand in Russian after being told that the revered Bolshoi Ballet meant only "Big Ballet", something which I have always found profoundly disappointing. Originally consisting of 10 assembly halls, one ordination hall and no less than 100 stupas, the temple is known to date back to 1292 and maybe before. There are stupas, classic bell shaped structures with a pointed top, that are still at their full height and others to which the years have been less kind. Like many such places, it has been added to, modified and more recently restored to some extent, though what is there now is much less than in its heyday. All the sites like this were well labelled and each one had an artist's representation of how it was thought to have been. It was fascinating to compare the ruins with their likely former glory and somehow easy to imagine this place as a functioning and busy habitation.

Numbers of Buddha figures were part of this particular site, sitting, standing and all looking serene. A bus had stopped nearby and disgorged a group of monks. While one of the things that made the place so special was how quiet it was, it was evocative to see the figures, their yellow robes toning in with the terracotta of the buildings they moved alongside, and from somewhere in the distance came the chanting sound of what were presumably more monks. There was already the occasional sound of a bell sounding somewhere else and the total picture all this presented seemed like a slice of history – well, as long as you ignored the bus.

Despite the impression the scenery gave, the heat hit me as I got out of the air-conditioned car. What must it have been like in this part of the world before the advent of air conditioning? I once stayed with a business colleague in his condominium apartment in Singapore. The spare bedroom had no air-con and, despite a fan, which I left on all night, I felt I hardly slept and the night seemed to last for ever.

I took time to walk around a number of the individual temples and buildings spread throughout the parkland. It was an atmospheric place, the peace and calm, presided over by innumerable Buddha figures all looking like contentment personified. The effect was enhanced by the fact that so few people were around; I could take in the atmosphere without interruption. Soon it was time for a cool drink and some lunch.

Although the area round about was quiet, the restaurant at its centre, a modern single-story building which looked incongruous amongst the ancient stone, was quite busy – by which I mean there were a couple of dozen customers. Three Thai girls, of perhaps 20 or so and who I guessed worked together, sat at a round table engaged in animated conversation. An American family came in and sat down nearby and the three children whispered together. The oldest was a boy of about 15 or16; the other two were girls. The boy kept taking surreptitious glances at the three Thai girls, all of whom were attractive and one of whom stood out and clearly grabbed his attention and his hormones. After some time eating and whispering, and despite the protests of her brother, the eldest girl spoke to the prettiest of the Thai girls who turned out to speak English.

"My brother would like your phone number. Will you give it to him?" The girl looked at her friends either side of her and giggled. "How old is he?" she asked. "Fifteen," came the reply. The three girls giggled some more, "No, no – too young. He need five more years," she said. The boy was blushing by now and moving away. The mother indicated that in any case it was time to go. As they all moved away, the father glanced back for a second. "And I suppose I'm too old," he said ruefully turning back to the family without waiting for an answer. His wife gave him a withering look, but by the time she spoke they were too far away for me to hear. It was probably something like, "One more remark like that and your holiday's over." The Thai girls watched them go and smiled and giggled some more. I ate a quick snack and moved on. There was a good deal to see but one place stood out for me.

*

People sometimes say they climb mountains "because they're there". I am more inclined to think that they do so more because no one else is there. Some places excite. Others, perhaps including mountain tops, induce calm and nothing offers a greater aid to relaxation than the right sort of personal "quiet place". Not that I have any difficulty relaxing. I am lucky enough (so my wife says) to be able to set aside the cares of the day and leave worries to one side if dealing with them is better done later rather than sooner. I tell her that may be so, but that I work at it. Never mind, there are occasions when even a relaxed soul like me finds their level of peace and calm extended by where they are. A walk may do it, not along a busy main road, certainly, but in the country, with a nice view and the prospect of a good pub at the end of the walk. Sometimes it is something more special: sailing my battered little boat on the estuary near my home takes me right away from everything. A whole day can go by with stunning views, only water birds for company and without having to do anything more taxing than wonder where the best place is to moor up for a sandwich lunch or which waterside pub to visit.

Now I have a new favourite "quiet place".

Set in the heart of Sukhothai, it is *Wat* Saphan Hin. This was top of my driver's recommendations, though he had not explained why, just saying enigmatically – *Must see, must climb*. The car pulled up at a small police point: a wooden hut not much larger than a telephone box with a small counter arrangement at its front. This is one of the areas of the park, entry to which necessitates paying a small fee; well, it's free if you are Thai, but being a mere *farang* I must pay. Having said that, the sum charged was tiny and the policeman told me that I should also take a bottle of water. I declined this, having just got out of an air-conditioned car, and the policeman said, in a way that proved prescient, "You have later". I did too.

The *Wat*, the name means "temple of the stone bridge", was approached up a long steep stretch of uneven steps. The first part was actually just a ramp, a path built up with rocks and stones with an increasing drop on either side. Half way up the path became irregular steps, but still needed a sure foot to mount it safely. It progressed, pretty much in a straight line until the ruined *wat* was reached some 300 metres above where the path started. The uneven path and the heat made it a disproportionately difficult climb. It was hot, just after midday, and there was no shade until the last few metres. And the way was steep, steeper as always seems to be the case with such things, than it looked from below. I was panting and sweating when I reached the top. The policeman had been right, I would need that water later; in fact I would have done well to bring it with me.

The ruins, maybe 30 metres by half that, were set side on to the approach; a carved stone Buddha more than 12 metres high, named *Phra Attharat*, stood looking down their length; another figure sat at his feet at the other end of the small square between them – both faces had smiles that seemed to indicate total contentment. Trees surrounded the site on the hillside above and cast rippling shadows over the stonework. Stone columns gave a clear indication of how the building here must once have been. Originally a monastery, the place made it easy to imagine orange robed monks going about their business in the shade of the trees. The standing Buddha's right hand was raised high and his palm faced outwards in a symbolic gesture that is believed to dispel fear and give protection.

It had seemed quiet in the area below. Up high, the quiet took on a whole new dimension. A solitary backpack-toting tourist had been sitting quietly reading as I arrived at the top; now he put the book away, acknowledged me in German and began the climb down, leaving me alone. I sat for a while on a stone wall looking out over the area below: its various buildings, statues and ruins, the tree-scattered landscape and the occasional signs of other visitors were all very much in the

Chapter Nine

distance. Everything seemed a long way off. The extreme serenity and quiet beauty of the place around me took over. I could have stayed there a very long time. If I could, I would return there whenever I needed to top up my measure of relaxation and calm.

Some places just exude atmosphere and this was one. I think even the world's greatest worrier would find their worries diluted by spending a few minutes there. The town I had set out from seemed a million miles away. I walked right around the place, sat down again, lost in the feeling of this special spot, hearing nothing except the sound of a light wind rustling the trees and making the orange silk draped around the Buddha figures' shoulders flap slightly. After some time I stood and walked to the edge, the start of the stone pathway leading down. Far below, the policeman was outside his small hut chatting to my driver; he waved. Then he returned to his hut, came out again holding a bottle of water and waved that. I am sure that, if we had been closer, we would have seen each other smile.

Eventually I picked my way slowly and carefully down the rough path and received the water gratefully.

"You need now," he said with certainty; and he was right. He knew he had been right as I arrived. He smiled as I slurped, and the Buddha figures above smiled on too. Maybe whoever carved them intended them to display calm and contentment, or perhaps over hundreds of years in such a place the look had gradually accumulated, as it were by osmosis, just because of the nature of their location. Certainly their tranquil smiles are an integral part of what makes the temple of the stone bridge worth the strenuous climb that visiting it entails.

Smile Because It Happened

*

As I continued around the park, I crossed paths several times during the day with a girl on a bicycle. In the full sunlight, the heat shimmered around her. I saw her making her way from patch of shade to patch of shade, making a wobbly stop at each new place she wanted to inspect. At each stop she dismounted, removed a huge sunhat and wiped her face with a large handkerchief, pulled out a bottle of water and gulped extravagantly; then she pulled out a sheaf of papers and guidebooks to look at alongside whatever she was viewing. Finally, I walked around a corner of one of the ruins and almost bumped into her. Her bicycle was leaning against a wall and she was sitting poring over a guidebook through large horn-rimmed spectacles, her head framed by a halo of curly hair. She was – how can I put this? Large. Well, actually she was very large. I had watched her from a distance settling onto the bicycle seat, her wide behind overlapping the seat on either side as she started up and pushed strenuously on the pedals, then undulating rather as a waterbed does if you drop something on it as she got under way. Nevertheless, despite not seeming to be designed for it, and despite the heat, I discovered that she had chosen to cycle around on her tour rather than opting for greater comfort. A low budget was not going to prevent her making the trip and seeing what she wanted to see and bikes were cheap to hire.

Melanie, as she proved to be called, was from North Carolina and on holiday from a teaching post in Korea. She told me that she had looked up heritage sites on the Internet and settled on this place as her target location.

Chapter Nine

"While I'm working in Korea I want to travel as much as possible in the region," she told me. "There is so much to see." She had been to numbers of places around the region, including Angkor Wat, the temple complex built for King Suryaraman II in Cambodia, and both of us had visited Burma, despite official policy to avoid visits that were said to support the military junta. She waxed lyrical about Bagan, the remains of a wooden city, the wooden buildings long gone, but apparently numberless pagodas left dotting the landscape and creating an iconic sight (one I wrote about in my book *Beguiling Burma*). Since then, discouragement of visiting has turned to some mild encouragement, but on meeting we debated the rightness of visiting, and both concluded that the reactions of people we had met, all of whom were clearly in favour, justified it. Uncharitably, I imagined this solitary trip being a compensation for the lack of any boyfriend in her life, but, be that as it may, she was passionate about history and loving every minute of her sweaty perambulations. Her approach seemed rather like the kind of bird-watcher known as a twitcher: that is, someone more motivated by being able to list record numbers of bird species spotted rather than by learning details about their lives. She was systematically working her way around the old city, ticking off each and every single place of any note. Yet she was clearly enjoying the experience, focusing on the details about each of her stopping places, and was determined to get to the bottom of her list despite the effort required to do so by bicycle. I wished her well. She took a final swig of water, wiped her forehead with her handkerchief again and mounted. The bicycle wobbled without any forward motion for a second or two – as did she – looking as if both she and

Smile Because It Happened

it might topple sideways rather than move forward. Then it edged forward an inch or two and then she was off, peddling onwards to her next scheduled stop.

Just watching her made me feel hot and I went back to the car for a drink. But her demeanour and her smile seemed to indicate an inner contentment with her chosen path that suited her well. Perhaps my thoughts about her not having a boyfriend were maligning her. Maybe he was waiting at home. Maybe she honestly did not want a partner in life or on her travels for the moment. Whatever the facts, for the moment, her decision to travel here on holiday was something she clearly regarded as a good one. It looked as if she would return to her teaching enriched by the experience; and, just possibly, a few pounds lighter too. I commented to my driver, "Nice lady," but he clicked the air con up a notch and said "Need more cool, less food". How unkind.

After two days of sightseeing (and in case you plan a visit here it could well justify taking up more time), I arrived back at the hotel in the early evening and went to take a final dinner there. No other restaurants were within walking distance, it had been nice on my first night and would do well again.

The hotel's restaurant, an area set to one side of the entrance courtyard, was partly inside, partly outdoors. It was a comfortable spot and a leisurely dinner would see some of the evening pass pleasantly. The two waitresses were clearly still at school and on duty as an evening job. They chatted and giggled together in a corner, leaping up every so often when a bell tinkled in the distance to announce that something was ready for its journey from the kitchen and dashing off to find and deliver it to the right table. I chose to sit outside, always a pleasure when climate allows, and here the heat of the day had

Chapter Nine

dissipated and it was a delightful warm evening. The tables were large, made of rough wood and with benches on each side, each able to seat eight people. On a normal evening, this was fine for groups or families, but space quickly filled up if several tables were occupied by a couple or a single person – in which case some sharing was necessary.

I sat down at such a table and looked at the menu, distracted only by one of the hotel's huge white rabbits, which sat a few yards away nibbling what looked like cabbage leaves. Soon it lolloped away, some spring rolls and a cold beer arrived and I began dinner. A man nodded to me and sat down at my table; this evening while the restaurant was not so busy, the fact that most guests were either solo or in couples meant sharing of tables was inevitable. I bade him good evening, but he only smiled and said, "No English". He ordered only a drink, downed it quickly and was soon departing, leaving me alone again at the large table.

Although I am comfortable traveling alone and with my own company, I had rather hoped he had spoken English. It would have been be nice to exchange a few words with one or more of my fellow guests. It was rather like waiting for an aeroplane to fill up, but in reverse. In the plane you are trying to identify undesirables and will them not to sit next to you; here, as a few newcomers drifted in, I wondered who might be interesting to sit with for a moment. I hoped that if sharing was necessary it was not someone to avoid.

It wasn't.

Chapter Ten

PLANS IN A COLD CLIMATE

*If you think you can, you can, and
if you think you can't, you're right.*
Mary Kay Ash

I had just ordered another beer when a Thai lady of perhaps 30 years old approached and asked if she could share the table, adding that the layout was "not good for small people"; this might not have been quite the right phrase, but it was clear what she meant. The non-English speaker had nodded as he left and I was happy to say hello to a replacement. Like so many Thais she was slightly built, and was also the sort of person who somehow radiated a look of being interesting, and she not only spoke pretty good English, but proved happy to chat.

As the balmy evening buzzed with cicada she told me her name was Noon – well, roughly. Her full name was beyond my pronunciation skills. She told me she was on a short trip with her parents, who were somewhat elderly and not in the best of health. Nevertheless they were enjoying the first holiday of their lives.

"They have never stayed in hotel before, they don't believe it," she told me. Tired out, they were in bed already after a day touring the area.

"Why this trip?" I asked. Initially she was reticent, saying something about hard times and the need to make up for it. Gradually she told me more. Her parents had a little land

Chapter Ten

outside a small town well to the north of Bangkok and made their living growing rice. She had an older brother and sister, about whom she said little, but gave the distinct impression that they were idlers. Noon was the one who had broken away; she went to university, worked her way through her course and got a degree in business administration. She had opened a small shop selling clothes – "fashion" – and began to do reasonably well, though she had been badly treated by a boyfriend: "Butterfly," she said, implying several women in his life, and would not elaborate. But then the family farm fell into difficulty. If I understood correctly, this was because her parents' increasingly frail health led to their not coping and the lack of any practical support from her brother and sister. In any event, the financial difficulties escalated and their land was repossessed by the bank.

She had seen herself as the only way to rescue the situation. Families are close in Thailand and the principle of helping others in difficulty is strongly held, but that does not mean that everyone has the resolve or ability to do something practical, or sufficient of those qualities to make a real difference in difficult circumstances. Doubtless many people do not and there is little back-up support – few of the kind of benefits that are available in most western countries exist. She resolved not just to help, but to do something to get their land back, indeed to buy it back outright.

She had a plan, the first of many as I was to discover. She had to earn more money. So she closed her shop, which supported her but could not do more than that, and moved to Bangkok. Almost the default position for many girls in difficulty in Thailand is to work in a bar. Initially, that is what she did. If she was to earn any amount of money then I suspect that doing so

Smile Because It Happened

must have involved her in more than just waitress duties. She mentioned the bar work, but understandably would say little more about it. "Not good, I could not do," she said. But she had an idea and she formed a plan.

I was soon astounded at her epic resourcefulness. She heard of someone, a friend of a friend, working in America. She checked it out. There, the level of earnings that was possible was apparently way beyond local possibilities and she reckoned a spell of work there would raise the necessary capital and enable the family land to be bought back and things put to rights. For many people, such a thought would doubtless be just a pipe dream: a friend of a friend, a country on the other side of the world; it was something that might sound good, but few people would act on it. Noon did. And when she told me exactly what she had done, and where she had gone, I was initially simply disbelieving.

She had gone to Alaska and, living in a tiny town on the coast, worked on a salmon fishing boat. I just could not imagine it, this slight young woman, who told me she had never been out of the country before, and thus had never before flown in a plane either, swapping the heat and outside life of Thailand for somewhere not only on the other side of the world but at the other extreme of climate. We complain about the winter weather in Britain, and life grinds to a halt if we have more than a couple of centimetres of snow, but Alaska experiences real winters. There, winter has a capital W. It is not just cold there, it is dangerously cold, with temperatures regularly way below zero. I checked a web site as I wrote this and the temperature that day was minus 22, and it can regularly be double that. This is more than enough to make even a large icicle shiver.

Chapter Ten

When I expressed utter disbelief, she produced some photos from her bag: in them she appeared all wrapped up in bulky clothes, wearing a hat and gloves and the background of the pictures was sea, snow and ice. The snow was, well, substantial does not begin to describe it – such snow must have been a revelation to someone who had previously never even seen a frost. In one picture, it was piled one storey high against one side of buildings in what appeared to be the modest high street of the little town. In another, the backdrop was a massive glacier. A picture of the fishing boat showed it surrounded by floating chunks of ice. Yet in every picture she was smiling. I imagined her exchanging emails with Alaska for the first time, seeing pictures of snow like this and yet not rejecting the idea out of hand as a quick route to freezing to death, but scraping together sufficient money for the airfare and setting off into the unknown.

On first arrival she had stayed with a friend of a friend, before getting her own tiny apartment. "What about the cold?" I asked. "It's okay. I get used to it," she said. "Many warm clothes." The photos she had shown me bore witness to the warm clothes, and her smile seem to indicate that she had indeed got used to it. She was effectively the housekeeper for the fishing boat, organising the supplies, cooking the meals – "big meals to keep everyone warm!" – and organising the routine and keeping the boat tidy on its trips to sea. "That's difficult," she said, referring to the tidiness, "but when they get used to me on board they do as I say." She smiled. I believed her. This was clearly one competent and feisty lady. She had done this for three years, spending some nine months in Alaska, so experiencing both winter and summer. On each visit she had undertaken a number of fishing trips, each lasting several weeks, and fitted in with the weather conditions, then returning home for a short spell back in Thailand with her family. Now the land was theirs again, and with things much better she had decided to take her parents on a brief holiday while she was in Thailand. "The plan now is to build a new house," she went on. "Is started." She had visions of a lovely traditional wooden Thai house. Another plan involved expanding the farm activities. "I want to grow pineapples," she said. Plans and more plans it seemed; any such venture would presumably need capital to buy the plants and get things going, but she seemed confident this would happen too.

All this was amazing enough, but it had had to be set up. When she had arrived stateside for the first time, her options had been limited and she had had to get a Green Card giving her formal permission to work in the United States. This had involved numerous journeys to Seattle and time-consuming battles with American bureaucracy and no doubt intimidating officials. I imagined some massive uniformed individual towering over Noon and failing utterly to imagine her on a salmon fishing boat. But, at this point, I was unsurprised that she had succeeded and got the necessary card. She was bright, intelligent, beautiful and clearly possessed a level of resolve way beyond that of most people. She personified the best of the pragmatic attitude that is typical of her nation's culture – indeed, she seemed to take it to new heights.

She explained that pay on the boat varied with the success of the fishing: "More fish, more money." Every member of the crew got an appropriate percentage of the income that a catch generated. The Thai girl she had stayed with initially had become a friend, there were several other Thai people in

Chapter Ten

the small town and they stuck together, spoke Thai amongst themselves and managed, with some difficulty over obtaining ingredients, to cook and eat some Thai food; indeed they sold some too as another money earner. They had even had a holiday – in Hawaii of all places. It seemed a long journey, but the Thai network gave them somewhere to stay and the flights were, she said, a "good price".

As we chatted, the revelations continued. I wanted to find out more. I ordered us another drink and had a dessert too, just to prevent the meal ending.

Noon told me that before going to Alaska she had changed her name, though I could not understand exactly what had prompted this: symbolic of a new start, perhaps. The process involved a trip to the temple and elaborate consultation with monks as to what name would suit her and, more important, what name would be auspicious for her future life; clearly, selecting something that the average *farang* could pronounce was not a consideration. This was followed by a legal process, the Thai equivalent of what in Britain is called changing your name by deed poll, I guess. That done, she had arranged to adopt her sister's daughter, not just to look after her, but formally, legally, to adopt. The sister she described only as "unreliable", though clearly it was unreliable with a big, bold capital U. Although her sister looked after the girl day to day, Noon believed that this new arrangement gave security for the future. Noon telephoned her "daughter" on a regular basis – "free on Internet" – and was determined to ensure she had a suitable role model and made a good life. It was yet another plan that seemed to be on track and she told me the girl, who was 14 years old, was doing well in school. I think Noon must have decided early on in life that she was going to do more than her simple rural background perhaps suggested was possible, and it seemed likely that her adopted daughter stood every chance of doing the same.

At this stage I would not have been surprised if she had told me she was going to run for parliament or be Thailand's first woman in space. I asked how many more times she would return to Alaska. "Not too many more, just until I have house and farm right," she said. I hoped that the current way of life she described would not continue forever. She confessed to missing Thailand, Thai ways and friends and family while in Alaska, but the circumstances had demanded something be done and, my goodness, she was doing it. Of all the things she could have done, going to Alaska seemed just about the least likely imaginable. Yet doing so had worked, and as one plan reached fruition she had others lined up to take its place. But what a step. How had she felt as she sat on the plane going off on that first trip, I had asked, but she was dismissive, saying only, "It's okay". Yet, despite the difficulties of what she was doing, she seemed content with her lot; indeed, when I expressed amazement at some of these revelations she shrugged, making a "what-else-would-I-do" gesture, as if everything she described was the most natural thing in the world. For her it seemed to be just that, and she appeared well satisfied with what she had achieved. As well she might be.

She really did make it sound like a good job. Far away and hard work certainly, and cold for sure, but there were nice people in the little town she lived in and she seemed to have a variety of sidelines, all clocking up the money she needed to build her house and see her plans to fruition. More photos showed that the building of her house, currently just the wooden frame was complete, was already under way. But

Chapter Ten

there were hazards too. Work on a fishing boat is hard and it can be dangerous. Once a careless crewman had swept her off her feet, turning as he held a long spar of some sort, and she had fallen to a no doubt wet and icy deck and cracked her head. Dazed, and bleeding copiously as head wounds tend to do, she had to direct her own rescue, while crew members recoiled at seeing her apparently at death's door. "I know where dressings are," she said "no one else can find." Although the cut was ultimately to prove not too bad, the captain summoned a helicopter – "Insurance pay," she explained – and she was winched aloft and flown to shore where a couple of stitches did the trick.

The next day the procedure was reversed. Back in the helicopter, she was flown out to the boat, and winched back onto deck "in time to cook lunch," she said, just as if this sort of thing was merely normal routine. Cook breakfast – sustain a head wound – apply temporary dressing – be winched to a helicopter – fly to hospital – get patched up – return… and cook steak and chips. No problem. Planting rice or harvesting pineapple, this job was surely not.

Meal over, we said goodnight and I wished her well. I had plans of my own: in the morning I had to catch a flight back to Bangkok. By the time I was up in the morning, the rented pick-up she was using for this short trip with her parents had gone. They were en route back to the farm and, for Noon, a few more days of warm weather before her next long flight back to the snow and ice, which she had told me was booked in a week or so. I trust she is still smiling despite the cold, a smile both determined and, given what she had achieved, of satisfaction; though I bet her goals simply move on ahead of her as one plan leads to another. Hearing her story certainly made me smile.

Chapter Eleven

TRANSPORT OF DELIGHT

Earth has not anything to show more fair.
**William Wordsworth (and used by
Michael Flanders in his song about buses)**

Thailand is a large country and many of its 60 million plus population seem to travel a good deal. Many people in Bangkok have family elsewhere in the country and such links spread far and wide. Of course, visiting family is only one of many reasons to travel and as a result the country has an extensive network of trains and buses. All work pretty well, though trains are slow, they seem to stop every few yards at small stations, and the nature of the roads, or many of them, keeps the long distance buses from breaking any speed records. You do not know the meaning of the word frustration until you have spent several hours on a two-lane country road in Thailand, endlessly stuck behind lumbering trucks spluttering noise and diesel fumes. In Bangkok the buses are much used, not many are air-conditioned and all are packed at most times of the day. They are also labelled in Thai script and it is very difficult for a stranger to work out which bus to get to where, though if you do, they cost only the equivalent of a few pence.

I have already mentioned Thailand's taxis: any visitor wary of these, or of the ubiquitous and surely more dangerous *tuk-tuk*, will find a range of cars available at hotels. Using the

Chapter Eleven

same driver regularly makes a difference too. There is one in Hua Hin who now always takes us to see his wife and two children when we first see him on a new visit; we are treated like old friends. The Skytrain has made a real difference to travel around Bangkok in recent years. Fast, efficient and air-conditioned, it may be regarded as "outrageously expensive" by locals, but for the visitor it is a bargain, well justified as you look down at the traffic below.

Amongst this profusion of transport options is another, which is much used. I discovered this only when invited to dinner in Hua Hin while on a brief visit to Bangkok. A long way to go for dinner, but I could fit it in and wanted to do so to meet up with good friends who I had not seen for a while. A taxi each way would have been a disproportionate cost, so I enquired about the minibuses, a form of transport I had seen and heard about but never previously used. "No problem," I was told. "Just go to Victory Monument, one every few minutes." I set off, taking the Skytrain to Victory Monument Station, which I found perched high above one corner of the wide square where Phahonyothin, Phaya Thai and Ratchawithi Roads meet to the north east of central Bangkok. The statue, a tall obelisk surrounded by carved figures representing the army, navy, air force and police, is heavily Western in design and commemorates the Franco-Thai war, a minor skirmish against French influence in Indo-China in 1940/41; this was in fact a brief and indeterminate affair, though Thailand won some territory in Cambodia and Laos – an outcome prescribed by the Japanese. Large and imposing though the monument is, its original purpose is rather lost: the territories gained were handed back as war ended in 1945 and the militarism of the period, the monument was erected immediately after the conflict in 1942, is now seen as inappropriate. It remains only as a conspicuous landmark.

Getting off the train and looking down to road level, at first I could see no sign of minibuses. At the top of the stairs leading down to the road a stall was set up selling some kind of orange fruit drink. A special promotion of some sort was on offer, for which the young seller had had her hair dyed bright orange, though whether this was in her contract or was just her idea to fit in with the spirit of things I have no idea. Whichever it was, it certainly drew attention to her; I wondered what colour she had asked for at the hairdresser: beverage orange, perhaps. She beamed as an apparent prospective customer approached her, but happily directed me to the right exit even though I did not buy a drink. Once at road level, only a few metres away, I found the series of tables she had described set up, mainly in small alleyways just off the street, and each bearing signs showing the name of a destination or two. Every destination you can think of, actually, and a whole raft of other places too. Certainly I could go to Hua Hin from here, or to Phuket or Pattaya, or dozens of other places including some way across the country. Journey times ran from an hour or so to 12 hours or more.

I duly bought a ticket and found I had timed it well – the next departure to Hua Hin, which had departures every half an hour, was only 10 minutes away. It was still early in the day, but already it was hot on the street and I climbed into the minibus, which was cool from its air conditioning, its engine running unattended in defiance of any worries about safety or global warming. Three other passengers were already in residence, all Thais. No English appeared to be

Chapter Eleven

spoken, my "Good morning" was acknowledged with nods and smiles, but also shrugs, which seemed to indicate "I cannot say more". Only two more passengers joined before we departed: a young man dressed in army uniform and a young women who appeared surgically attached to her mobile phone and engaged in a series of long calls throughout the journey. Unusually she did so speaking quietly with her hand cupped over her mouth, though whether this was to avoid annoying her fellow passengers or to preserve confidentiality I do not know; in any case as everyone else dozed most of the way, no one was listening.

For 15 minutes after pulling into the road we travelled a total distance of perhaps quarter of a mile as the solid traffic around us edged slowly forward; then, just as I was preparing myself for a long haul and wishing I had brought a longer book, we took a left turn and were clear of the jam. We slowed, stopped so that the driver could pay a toll and were on the expressway. There is an extensive toll highway system in and around Bangkok these days, something that must, I suppose, ease the traffic somewhat, though it often appears otherwise and jams are the norm in many areas. Go to such an area and ask a child if the traffic ever flows freely nearby, it is said they will say, "I don't know, I'm only six". This time, since I had last visited, a new option had been introduced with toll payment: drivers could get what was called an Easy Pass, which automatically triggered payment in special lanes and the pass bearers could move through quickly. Unfortunately, as yet few people had such passes, which meant that the special lanes now used for pass holders were virtually empty while queues were extra-long at all the other lanes. Later I asked a taxi driver about the new passes. He laughed out loud, finding the whole idea of paying out for a pass in advance absurd. His passengers paid as they went; maybe the system will bed in after some time and things will speed up. Nevertheless, once this toll was paid our progress was good from then on.

I watched our surroundings as we gradually left the city. Soon we were passing miles of flat countryside. Some livestock was in evidence, primarily cows: Thailand seems to specialise in very skinny looking creatures with a hint of water buffalo about them. They look as if they are starving, but I am always assured it is "just how they are". Other fields have crops of many sorts from rice to pineapple, though almost all the way there were also signs of habitation with houses, shops, workshops and more lining the road. Recently, the main road to Hua Hin has been improved and for much of the way the local traffic is now separated from the through traffic, making life easier for both. Some of the traffic is very much part of the local scene: amongst the predominantly Japanese cars I saw a plethora of trucks of all shapes and sizes, many with loads that seemed to defy both the laws of gravity and any reasonable safety standard . With even a glance at the traffic one quickly comes to the belief that most Thais run small businesses that demand they drive a pick up. There are thousands of them, some open backed, some covered. Many of these carry tall, swaying loads; indeed, at several points along the road, police check points stopped some of the more precariously loaded, though what they did then I don't know. Imposed a fine perhaps, but did the driver also have to unload the top third of a towering load of say pineapples and abandon them at the roadside? Somehow I rather doubt it.

Chapter Eleven

It is usual for pickups to carry people, sometimes lots of people and often they appear just to sit on the flat metal floor at the back. On this journey, one thing I had not seen before was pickups with a row of hammocks fastened from side to side from the high rails along the truck's rear section. In these people slept, apparently soundly, as their hammock swayed in time with the movement of the vehicle. Safety may not rank as high here as the standards now routine in Western countries, but practicality does – such ideas just seem to work.

Our driver drove fast, but well, and clearly knew the road in every detail: occasional, apparently mysterious moments when he slowed down always quickly showed themselves to be well judged, as a pot hole or other hazard appeared in front of us, and were then circumvented with precision. Other hazards were less predictable: twice we swerved to avoid a dog – dogs that is, it was not the same one each time. And we also had close encounters with a steaming wok on wheels and a ponderously moving cow that seemed not to have a care in the world despite being passed by vehicles on every side as it perambulated through the traffic. I hope it made it across safely, but maybe someone had steak for dinner.

After only two hours and 10 minutes, a time that many a taxi might find hard to match, we pulled into a small yard off the main road in the centre of Hua Hin. No stops, no hassle and almost no money – the fare was less than *baht* 200. No wonder Thailand is a backpacker's paradise: if they have the time, visitors can roam the entire country with transportation so cheap, indeed, if you go on a bus, and maybe one without air-conditioning, the fare will be even lower. Fares here match the travel method, with greater comfort demanding a greater investment. Perhaps the lowest cost option I have ever come across in the region was in Thailand's northerly neighbour, Burma. There, pick-up truck "buses" ferried absurd numbers of people around with those on the outside clinging on for dear life; I was assured that when it was so full that some people could only hang on with one hand, they were only charged half price. There too an option even less costly was a cart pulled by bullocks. In comparison with that my Hua Hin minibus was sheer luxury. I would recommend these to anyone.

*

What about more personal transport? Bangkok's traffic, legendary for its chaotic and often unmoving nature, drifts around the city and beyond with the attendant exhaust fumes creating the almost permanent smog that so often hangs low in the sky. When I first visited the city the majority of the vehicles on the road were very old, all taxis were without air-con and jams and fumes were worse even than they are now. Then and now, given the comparatively low average income of much of the population, the only possible transport of choice for many people is a motor bike.

In the West, a motor bike is what overtakes you on a blind corner travelling at well over the legal limit and giving you are a near heart attack as it swerves to avoid oncoming traffic. There are those who think that God only allowed the motor bike to be invented to rid the world of a certain kind of reckless youth, though not all motor bike riders are young. There are also those in middle years who, perhaps unable to finance a meno-Porsche, ride with equal abandon. In

Chapter Eleven

Thailand, motor bikes are the transport of choice of the ordinary guy. There are thousands of them, and amid the chaos of any street, perhaps as you sit depressed and unmoving in yet another jam, they somehow do move, slipping between the lines of traffic and continuing to make their way along, albeit slowly. And as they go they can often raise a smile.

If your only means of transport is a small, noisy bike trailing a cloud of smoke, you make the best of it. You use it and you use it for anything and everything. This is evident with regard to family, friends and in many cases business activities too, and no allowance appears to be made for quantity or weight. I have often seen small bikes carrying two adults and three children, sometimes more. The suspension, if any is left, seems to cope, though some bikes ride noticeably low to the road. One common configuration is a man driving, with a woman riding pillion and most often sitting side-saddle in what appears to be a very precarious manner. Young women, usually in short skirts and high heels seem to ride in this way without thought or worry or indeed sometimes without even holding on, but the number of parcels they will often carry maybe makes doing so impossible. What is even more amazing is the number of girls who ride in this way while doing something else: talking on the telephone, filing their nails and, even on bumpy roads, applying makeup. All seem possible. Helmets still seem largely optional, though they are I think a legal requirement and, in the city at least, the majority of riders wear one. I am told the accident rate is high, indeed I was once told that the Thai word for motorcyclist is the same as that used to describe a suicidal person.

Smile Because It Happened

If a bike does crash, it will shed more than people. The loads carried are often huge and surprising. They are piled high and arranged fore and aft; I have seen bikes carrying long flexible pipes, a dozen of them, five times longer than the bike and bobbing up and down at either end as they go. Animals feature often: live pigs in cages, chickens and ducks in reed baskets or, if dead, then hung by their feet from poles; fish packed in ice, the ice leaving behind a trail of melted water on the road as they go. Ice also features simply as a cargo en route to bars and restaurants. In a hot country this is big business, and by European standards Thailand is hot all the time. In England you can miss summer completely if you have a day in bed. I have never seen where the ice comes from – a cube-isserie perhaps. Also in evidence is a huge range of fruit and vegetables. Other cargo too is just not what you would expect to see on a motor bike and, while all these amazing loads can raise a smile, some are just bizarre: they include a man transporting tyres simply by placing them over his head to make a pile so high that he has to strain to raise his head sufficiently to see where he is going over the top one. His arms protrude between the pile to allow him to grip the handlebars. On another occasion I saw a bike loaded with three piles of boxes of eggs, with the top of the stack behind the rider way higher than his head. Yet presumably breakages must be minimal or surely the economics of transporting eggs by bike would rule this out. This last image stays with me and returns every time I have eggs for breakfast in a hotel in Thailand; perhaps some arrive at their destination as ready-made omelettes.

These sights are repeated everywhere you go, both in the city and in rural areas where the picture is enhanced when bikes negotiate undulating tracks and weave past obstructions ranging from construction work to strolling dogs and cattle. The situation goes up the scale too: people who ride a *tuk-tuk* often load it to impossible heights and trucks of all sizes groan under their towering loads. All this imaginative loading is undertaken as if it is the most normal thing in the world, yet if you catch a rider's eye, raise an eyebrow or make a comment about a load – perhaps as it stops next to your taxi at a traffic light –the driver will usually grin and respond in a way that shows that he is all too well aware that he is pushing the limits.

Any near accident is greeted in the same way. An unexpected pothole may shake a load, allowing it to survive and cling on only by a whisker; if so, the rider will always respond by smiling to himself and to anyone else who happened to witness the near mishap. The only motorbike accident I have witnessed did not involve a cargo, but a bike crossing a four lane road in a bid to turn into a small side road – a *soi*. The rider misjudged the manoeuvre and clipped the rear wing of the taxi I was riding in, toppling off and sliding along the road for some distance. My driver stopped immediately as did a number of cars round about. He got out slowly, going first to inspect his rear wing and, having reassured himself that no great damage had been done, only then going over to the motor cyclist who by then was struggling to his feet. No great harm seemed to have been done to him either. It was treated in a way that indicated such things were a regular part of life on the road and everyone was soon back on their way. Motorcycles are dangerous in Thai traffic, however. An American friend, who teaches in Bangkok, used one for many years, then was hit by a truck, which pulled out onto a main road at night without looking and went straight into him. He had a knee repaired with metal pins and hobbled on crutches for many months; he used the time to plan the purchase of a car.

As we drove on, the driver had to brake as another man, probably in his early 20s, ran across the road in front of him, jumped the central barrier and wove his way across the other carriageway, dodging traffic and accompanied by a screaming of brakes. A few yards ahead, a policeman, who had evidently decided not to give chase, stood by his bike speaking into his radio. It's not just the traffic itself that slows your progress in Bangkok, it's all that goes with it.

Like so much else in Thailand, driving motorbikes is done the Thai way. Perhaps the habitual degree of overloading should be outlawed. I am sure that Health and Safety officials in many a Western country would have a field day if anything similar happened under their jurisdiction – "A dozen eggs is one thing, sir, but 10 dozen and those car tyres: no way." But here it is ever present and seems likely to remain so. It's just necessary, it seems to work, indeed to work well and, besides, without it journeys through Thailand would lose just a little of their smile-inducing fascination.

Wherever you want to go in this country, there will be a way of getting there, probably many different ways in fact and, whatever means you select, the journey itself is likely to be entertaining.

Chapter Eleven

Chapter Twelve

EATING, RAINING, FEETING

Food is an important part of a balanced diet.
Fran Lebowitz

The number of people visiting Thailand has climbed, over the years, hardly surprising in my view given the nature of the place. However, the growth of tourism has also suffered from repeated setbacks, and some of those might be best described as own goals in a one step forward, two back kind of way.

The first of these to mention was no own goal, it was nature in the raw: the tsunami that hit Thailand, and other parts of South East Asia, at Christmas time in 2004. It killed many more than 10,000 people, including a large number of tourists, and many more were injured. Property damage was considerable. Pictures were dramatic and tourist numbers dropped immediately, indeed they have as yet never reached the same heights again. Many of the famous name holiday spots in Phuket and elsewhere were affected; the worst hit was probably *Kho Lak* where predominately low-rise holiday accommodation was swept away. The effect was fickle in its geography. Siripan's son, Pub, worked at the time in Phuket at a beachside hotel. Here water came up the beach, but only just touched the hotel, yet a bay less than a couple of kilometres away was one of the worst hit places. The disaster was bad of course, but the press always dramatise these things: for instance, Phuket is more than 60 miles long, but only a tiny

Chapter Twelve

part of its coastline was affected. Yet you could easily have been led to believe that the entire island had been swamped.

The details of the disaster have been well documented elsewhere, but recovery was, for the most part, well handled, though there were reports of fishermen being cheated out of land their families had lived on for generations by developers riding roughshod over their lack of correct documentation to prove ownership. Certainly the Thai habit of pulling together helped. My wife and I arrived in the Kingdom a day or two after the event and a while later my wife was talking to a lady giving her a pedicure at the beachside. She told us how she had sent a parcel of clothes, rice and other things to help those affected. She could not have earned much money and we said how good it was of her to do this. She replied very simply, "Everyone do same".

The effect of this on numbers visiting lingered and has been made worse by various political shenanigans; even mildly unruly demonstrations resulted in more cancelled holidays. In June/July 2010, more political protests of the sort that have regularly dogged Thai life took place in the capital and elsewhere. The worst were close to Silom Road, one of Bangkok's business and shopping districts. For much of the time the protest was peaceful: like the occupation of the airport a year or more before, it involved women and children, music, dancing and eating. It did develop a nasty edge towards the end: shots were fired, a few buildings were set on fire and around a hundred people were killed as police finally moved in to clear the paralysis it had brought to the streets for more than two weeks.

With instant media coverage, pictures of such events flash quickly around the world focussing, of course, on the excesses and the worst of what is going on and with accompanying headlines that, however they are phrased, say to prospective visitors of all sorts, "Danger. Think twice before visiting Thailand". Whatever political grievances may exist, and there are certainly some, you would think protesters of whatever persuasion, all declaring their love of their country, would find a better way to protest than this immediate own goal, which has tourism figures spiralling down like water down a drain. Maybe something that would affect politicians personally rather than thousands and thousands of people caught in the downdraft, as it were. Letting the tyres down on their smart limousines would probably not be enough, but there must be something: less chanting of slogans and more creativity, please, protestors, and we *farangs* would be more likely to visit your country without misgivings.

The reduction in foreign visitor numbers at such times is dramatic overall, but of course it has an individual effect on countless people. Small shops and businesses nearby that demonstration were forced to close and large corporations were affected too. I have a friend who is on the management team at a hotel situated just a few hundred metres from the protest just described. At one point during that time, only three of their 400 or so rooms were occupied. Police helicopters clattered around their roof top, smoke and on occasion tear gas swirled along the road outside, and the threat of worse to come was all pervading. In addition, the hotel had their gas supply, on which they cooked, cut off. Food for their few guests and any other people who did venture in was cooked elsewhere and finished off on site so as to keep any small level of business going. "It's okay. We find a way," I was told, but revenue dropped massively and some

Chapter Twelve

members of the staff were laid off with no pay, something that is evidently a normal and permitted response to such a situation, while others who were needed to continue working had to do so on a reduced salary. Yet it was the positive side of all this that people described: "We kept going", "We did not close", "We made sure our customers okay". Customers may have been few, but okay I'm sure they were. Even when describing a week or two with no pay, people smiled. There was a "had-to-be-done" feeling about it all and, of course, once the situation changed the staff rallied and put everything back in order again.

*

Just like the tsunami, some other hazards can neither be predicted nor easily controlled and are certainly not own goals, though the negative impact on tourism is the same. In October 2011, I flew into Bangkok and looking out of the window for the last 20 minutes or more of the flight as we descended towards the airport, I saw the landscape below, which is usually countryside and farmland, was predominantly water. Buildings were visible, the borders of some fields were clear, but most roads were presumably flooded as there appeared to be none. This was part of the massive floods following an exceptional monsoon season that engulfed a large area of the country. It got worse over the next few weeks and only abated as the rains stopped, the temperature won and things dried out. The atmosphere in the city was decidedly untypical; it was an odd time to be a visitor.

One result of the rapid abandonment of some homes is that numbers of pets, dogs and cats are left to their own devices. Largely this is unintentional, though the papers reported one man caging a dozen dogs and leaving them to drown. An animal rescue outfit had stepped in and saved them, though they had hesitated to do so as it meant breaking into private property. Rightly so, as it happened, as after the rescue they were promptly faced with a law suit. I hope it came to nothing and common sense prevailed: how cynical can you be? Though perhaps the dog's owner, having lost his house, felt no opportunity to get something back could be missed. More serious, surely, was the loss of livestock upon which peoples' livelihoods depended.

The city centre where I was staying was dry, but being curious I went to the river by Taksin pier where various hotels on the far bank have boats running a regular ferry service to and from their properties. To one hotel I know – the Anantara – the boat ride is usually a little more than 20 minutes in duration. That day it took eight. The second the boat left the jetty it was swept downstream by the swollen waters and the current accelerated still more where a bridge narrowed the channel. Beforehand as I waited for the boat to arrive, something crashed about in the undergrowth alongside the jetty and a huge crocodile rushed out across the planking. Its jaws snapped only a few feet from me and… no, of course that did not really happen, though one of the rumours rife in the city was that not just dogs had been abandoned to the flood waters, but more exotic pets including those likely to wreak havoc on the population when freed. Just a rumour, I'm sure, though in Bangkok you never know and certainly snakes normally living in rivers and *klongs* might well have moved to flooded areas where people were wading through the water.

Chapter Twelve

Two feelings about all this seemed to prevail. First, people were essentially philosophical about the flood and about how much worse it might get. They seemed to prefer to assume that all would be well… until it wasn't. Shops, offices and other buildings varied in their preparations. Some had built breezeblock walls two or even three feet high across their frontages, others had massive arrays of sandbags and stacks ready to fill any gaps left for people to enter when the water came, if it did. Others, though, had done nothing, and a surprising number had an incomplete row of single height sandbags across their doorsteps that would clearly make absolutely no difference to their plight.

Many people, of course, had already been affected. My hotel had staff with homes already flooded staying in some of their rooms; work evidently must go on, certainly in a hotel. One staff member I spoke to said, "What can we do? Only can move upstairs, but have one floor only." Families were pulling together and much sharing was spoken of – how long all this might last people had no idea and confidence in government predictions were about as low as the regard in which Western bankers now seem to be held. Already major damage had been done: Bangkok's second airport had suspended operations as water lapped around the planes' wheels and whole factories were underwater – Honda was one large company badly affected. And, of course, tourists were cancelling in droves, though holiday areas such as Hua Hin on the east coast and Phuket and other islands were safe enough, as were other cities such as Chiang Mai in the north of the country. However, tourist attractions such as the ancient city of Ayutthaya north of Bangkok were cut off and pictures from rural areas and small towns across the whole area north of Bangkok were very off-putting.

Later, as I left to return to London, it was sufficiently quiet for me to speak to the lady who stamped my passport; I had got into the habit of expressing sympathy and asking people if they had been affected. I expressed hope that her home was okay. We must have held up people arriving behind me as she immediately told me that no, it was not – water was chest high in the one storey building in which she lived. She stood up behind her counter and ran her hands over her body. "All my clothes I wear," she said. "Just uniform. Nothing more left." There were tears in her eyes as I mumbled inadequately and moved past her into the departure area. What were such people to do? Certainly not working and not getting paid would just make their situation worse. Huge numbers of people somehow found time to help others, either because their own homes were okay or they could leave work (or there was no work).

Of course friends and family pulled together. Only one thing was certain at that point: a huge amount of water was currently north of the city and would pass south to the sea one way or another. If this draining off occurred slowly, and if various barriers and defences held, it might not get worse, but the worst case scenario was a meter of water right across down town Bangkok. If I had been scheduled to fly home later than I was, there would have been a real chance of travel becoming very difficult.

Traffic in the city was already affected. Why? Obviously where roads were under water, but this was not the case with central areas and the expressways. The latter, mainly raised high above the level of the city streets, had the inside lane

Chapter Twelve

blocked by parked cars right along much of their length. Those living in threatened areas were not going to risk their precious vehicles being written off. The lane alongside moved slowly too as more people looked for parking places. The scale of this illegal parking had overnight become impossible to police and was being tolerated with Thailand's normal pragmatism. Can you imagine the glee that such a situation would cause in London, or indeed elsewhere in U.K.? The traffic wardens would think all their Christmases had come at once as they rushed from car to car, affixing penalty tickets and exerting their power. There would be a rash of clamping, towing and fining akin to sharks having a feeding frenzy. And I bet tolerance would be in short, short supply – "I know the warning sign is underwater and you can't see it, but you still get a ticket." I bet, too, that contesting a fine and writing to the council to say that your house and drive were underwater would do you no good at all, even if the flood had been compounded, as many claimed in Bangkok, by officials being slow to react and take mitigating measures.

I followed the story after I left. The flooding got a little worse, but the city centre remained dry. Tens of thousands of people were affected, however. A friend working for the hotel I stayed in kept me posted: she had a day off to work with neighbours to protect their houses with sandbags, more staff moved into the hotel, but the sand bags stacked around the hotel entrance were not needed, her house remained safe and gradually the situation improved. It would doubtless take a good while for all those things and people who were affected to recover. The story, as is the way with such things, quickly dropped out of the international news, though the implications would remain for quite a while, even if, as so often, Thai people smiled their way through it. In fact, three months on newspaper reports were saying little remained to show what had happened, though I suspect that this applied primarily to what tourists would see; some places certainly retained evidence of the flood. A home destroyed would certainly leave a mark. The ancient city of Ayutthaya was one of the few tourist sites flooded, thought it reopened quite quickly. Dead vegetation still bears testament to the damage and the ruins of ancient temples now have a high-tide mark. Restoration work was in evidence as the Fine Arts Department worked busily to restore the place's former glory.

But life goes on and the rapid leaving of the problem behind is another sign of the Thai philosophy on such matters. The manager of the Oriental Hotel in Bangkok, itself unaffected, was quoted as saying, "People here only deal with problems when they are upon them. When problems are gone they are also gone from everyone's minds. This thinking is an integral part of Thai culture." Or, as a Thai said to me, "Now today more important."

*

Thai food is a legend in its own mealtime. From the simplest establishments (one of my favourites is little more than an open-sided thatched roof on the beach) to the more formal and the frankly grand, all have one thing in common. As well as the meals they serve they offer a special welcome and friendly service. Whether the initial greeting is a few words in rudimentary English or, as with another of my favourite restaurants, a hug for regular customers from the smiling lady who runs it and an update on her life since you last visited, it

Chapter Twelve

is always a pleasurable part of the whole experience. This is true on a first visit and even more so on making any subsequent ones. Welcoming you back takes on more friendly overtones and conversation can then begin to range far and wide, certainly way beyond the food and your order.

Even the international chains are different here. At a Swenson's outlet, one of a chain of what used to be called ice cream parlours, specifically the one located behind Bangkok's excellent Anantara Resort & Spa, I was once greeted by the words, "Do you have a reservation?" This seemed bizarre for such a place; we wanted an ice cream not a three course meal, for goodness sake, but it was early on a Saturday evening, the place was packed and many customers evidently really did make reservations. I guess if it keeps the customers flowing through, this is only sensible. Faced with four *farang* clearly bemused by such a situation, the young man, who looked as if he had served his apprenticeship in McDonalds and was now pleased to be able to make some decisions, quickly switched to "Okay, okay. We'll fit you in," and, smiling broadly, he did just that.

Rarely is any lack of fluency in English allowed to dilute the welcome given. Just a smile and the offer of a menu can speak volumes. Smiles certainly say, "Hello and welcome", "Welcome back" or "Good to see you again". Maybe they also say, "Thank goodness, just as well some people come back or we would be out of business" or, who knows, even on occasion, "Amazing, despite this being a gastronomic hell hole someone has actually come back – please come in". In fact few Thai restaurants lack the quality to make this last one likely.

At the beach restaurant I mentioned earlier, the welcome is first to the beach. You are shown to beach loungers (use of them is free if you eat at the restaurant), offered drinks, weather reports and comments on other visitors – "Very fat. Swedish. They come every day, but always eat chips" – this comment made with amazement that anyone could intentionally spurn Thai food. Settling you in involves finding out how much sun and shade you want, how close to the sea you want to be and then, once you are settled, comfortable and with just the view of the sea you want, a tab is started, drinks are brought and you can pay when you leave the beach later in the day.

Want to take a walk by the shore? Just let them know and they will keep an eye on your things. Want something to eat? Just move to the tables under the thatched roof and closer to the kitchen and... enjoy. Yet I notice that few customers seem to talk much to the staff. This could be only because they speak little English; many of those on the beach in question typically come from Scandinavia and right across Europe as well as from the U.K. But if you do chat to them it is welcomed. You can discover which waiter (a grand name for servers in such a setting) fancies which waitress, when the best prawns will be in – indeed their whole life history if you wish. Such conversations can be interesting, informative and fun – a way for the visitor to learn more about a place and its people.

So many people you cross paths with in Thailand seem happy to talk and, whether it is just a remark or two or a life history, it is often interesting and can raise a smile. This seems often to be the case in restaurants and cafés. For example, I once went into a café hoping to buy some jam, I like to take one or two sachets with me on a plane journey to liven up their rolls. I asked if they had such a thing and was assured they had. I asked if I could buy two or three "for my flight". The man behind the counter said very seriously, "Oh so sorry I cannot sell to you", then breaking into a wide smile as he set three down on the counter. "I give to you, no problem."

The owner of a small café near a hotel in Phuket where we had breakfast in an environment rather like theatre as local people came and went, told us she had just bought the business after living in the United States for 25 years and working as a dealer in a casino. "Now semi-retired," she said, putting on more eggs, catching toast as it popped out of the toaster and pouring coffee at the same time. It looked like quite a job to me, despite her willing team of waitresses, one of whom appeared with a new hair style one morning and told us it was "So you can remember me being sexy," despite "Me old – 26". Asked if it would win her a new boyfriend, she seemed to settle on something meaning – chance would be a fine thing, but who knows. From next door a beautician came out for coffee to where we were sitting outside under an umbrella, and also joined in. "I have no boyfriend for many years," she said. "No need. Can go to supermarket and buy batteries". Perhaps more optimistically, a young guy went by wearing a T-shirt that said "Tonight I am single". The path to true love is clearly a rocky one.

*

I love eating on the beach in a country where the climate actively suggests it. Coming from Europe, one thing always puzzles me. There always seems to be an odd absence of birds on Thailand's beaches, certainly compared to the profusion on the estuary outside my window at home. Given the food on them, an abundance of crabs and the odd marooned fish, and surely a cornucopia of worms and the like below the sand, I am not sure why this is. There are certainly no seagulls, indeed any birds you do see are not sea shore ones. Two raise a smile, however. First there is what I have come to call the "clean-up pigeons". It's a pigeon-like bird, certainly it walks with a pigeon-like gait, and has little fear of people. There always seem to be a few about whenever you eat outside. Drop even a crumb or a grain of rice and they are there to dispose of it in a second. In this restaurant there are sparrows too. They have one trick I have not seen before: they had found a dripping tap and a dozen or so lined up sitting in a neat row underneath it, each then taking turns to cock their heads and catch the drips as they fell at the rate of one every couple of seconds or so. I doubt that sparrows are capable of giving a cheeky smile, but these gave every impression that they would do so if they could.

A similar situation exists in many kinds of establishment: pubs, restaurants large and small, big hotels and small guest houses. Even in a large hotel, where the throughput of large numbers of customers might be presumed to distance staff and guests to a greater extent, the level of involvement can be substantial. This is different to the level of actual service – that is certainly generally good in Thailand; for instance, I find that the way in which one is recognised on return visits – even after a long time – is extraordinary. Of course, some of this is the system. Check in for the second or third time at many a hotel and something will appear on the computer flagging that you have been there before and they can say, "Nice to see you here again" whether they physically

Chapter Twelve

recognise you or not. I know one hotel where a regular guest will be asked if a photograph may be taken of them; then this is circulated to each department and whenever you visit you will find yourself recognised everywhere you go in the hotel. Another hotel, already mentioned here earlier – the famous Oriental in Bangkok – takes photos of the rooms occupied by their most important regular guests and then uses them to ensure that everything is arranged just so for their next visit.

Another favourite of mine is a small hotel on the coast. It is owned by a family of seven; six brothers and a sister. A family atmosphere prevails. One brother runs the hotel, his wife handles all the administration, another brother visits regularly, still other siblings visit occasionally. Arrival can swamp you in a delightful barrage of greetings and smiles if many family members happen to be around. Then there are the members of staff. The girl on reception beams a welcome and wants to know how you are, the guy who takes the suitcases to the room adds his two-pennyworth and you ask about his family. He is married to one of the girls in the restaurant and they have an adorable little daughter who will doubtless be brought to see you later in your stay. On our last visit a sister had arrived. When he and his wife first got together he kept speaking of it, but it was not clear who was the object of his affections. We asked. He replied that she was the one that is "small and beautiful". But they all were; further investigations were necessary. His wife and her colleagues will add to the welcome when you go for a drink and other staff will gather round to see how you are and welcome you back. People sometimes ask why I like returning to a place rather than exploring new pastures, though actually I like to do that too. The answer, in Thailand at least, is easy. It is because of the way you are treated and the involvement that just a little initial conversation can start in train. The experience is enhanced time by time as your experience and involvement grow, and good service gives way to friendship.

Food on holiday is a hazard. Too much and it is not just your suitcase that is overweight when you travel home. I find breakfast is a great luxury when staying in a hotel, not least just having the time if you are on holiday to linger over it. Incidentally, there is one safeguard to weight gain when taking the tempting buffet breakfast often offered at a hotel: you walk it off. In some larger hotel the breakfast layout gets you covering miles, threading your way through other tables to the buffet and back on a regular basis. What is more, some of this is totally unnecessary. In many a hotel you are first shown to a table and, almost always, to reach it you pass the buffet and disappear into the distance, sit down and then promptly realise you must get up and walk back. The smiling waitress may have shown you to a table, but she is not going to bring you any food; the weight-loss-or-weight-gain trek begins. In other establishments the room is more modestly proportioned and unscheduled exercise is minimised, though maybe the keenest guests can opt to sit somewhere else, walking to and fro to the beach perhaps and triumphantly noting the number of steps taken on their activity sheets. Or maybe the initial greeting should be not just "Tea or coffee?" but "Pedometer?"

Usually you will be welcomed at any hotel or restaurant, of whatever kind and size, and service is universally good in my experience. Sometimes, if things should go wrong, then a smile is the best way forward. The Thais value a reasonable, pleasant approach so, if you are bumped off a flight, arrive at

Chapter Twelve

your hotel to find your booking got lost in cyberspace or your chosen dish arrives with fins instead of claws, never rant and rave. Rather, smile and politely seek someone's cooperation in sorting things out. Many times I have witnessed the shutters go down, as it were, as someone new to Thailand launches into an aggressive row, coming on strong in an attempt to sort something out, when this all too easily makes things worse.

Sometimes service extends as frankly heroic efforts are made to assist. I have Australian friends who checked out of their small hotel in Chiang Mai, one delightfully located on the river and with a courtesy boat that goes to the town centre rather than a bus. They then found that their flight back to Australia, one involving a change before they reached their home city, had been unceremoniously cancelled. Despite the fact that the bill was paid, someone from the hotel offered to help. They made suggestions, actually went with them to a travel agent and also to an airline office and did not leave them until they had a suitable alternative all set up and safely confirmed. No charge, no hesitation and a smile accompanying the whole thing.

*

Thailand is a good place to shop, not only for its own special items, silk, pewter, handcrafts, silver and other jewellery, but almost anything now Bangkok has major shopping centres to match any in the world. I am not a good guide to most kinds of shopping, though I have an eye for a bargain and as I have regularly visited in January (November to March being the best months weather-wise: cooler and dryer than other seasons, though it is always hot by European standards), I hardly own a shirt that does not come from Thailand and was not bought in their January sales.

If I must go to a large shopping centre, because I love books, bookshops always make me smile and provide a refuge while my wife does other things. I like nothing more than having time to browse, especially if I discover something new to me amid the blandness of the ubiquitous 3-for-2 offers so favoured by most stores these days, or better still something both new to me and unusual. In my view, there are few more important elements of travel planning than selecting the right books to pack and selecting what is just right for whiling away time in airports, on flights, buses or wherever else you need to be removed from whatever unpleasant or irrelevant activity may be going on around you; or indeed just to relax awhile on the beach or over a solitary meal.

So, even if I have carefully selected titles in my suitcase (or loaded on my Kindle), a trip to a big bookshop is irresistible. The one at Bangkok's huge, glossy, multi-storey Paramount shopping centre at Siam Square must be one of the largest bookshops in Asia. It is modern, well stocked and full of smiling assistants who actually know where things are located; there is a small coffee shop, too, that sells excellent cake. It offers an oasis amidst the plethora of fashion stores and everything else, even including a Porsche dealership set up on the fourth floor. There are, in fact, showrooms for several brands of upmarket car here so, unless they bring their stock in and out after hours, perhaps one needs to be careful not to be run over while shopping as well as not to be seduced into buying something unwanted by the sheer exuberance of the place. If shopping tires you there is a huge food court in the basement.

Chapter Twelve

So, into the bookshop I go and, on one occasion, after a while wandering around, I found something I wanted to make a note about. I had promised a friend that I would let them know the author of two books about China that I had read and recommended to them. *The Great Wall* and *The Terracotta Army* are, I discovered, by one John Man. I went to the counter, obtained some paper – in fact a bookmark – and borrowed a pen to make a note. I wandered on, quickly discovering something else worth noting and took up the bookmark a second time, then realised again that I still unaccountably had no pen with me. Across the table of books I was alongside was a smartly dressed lady wearing a shiny, brass-coloured name badge; she was carrying a clipboard and making notes. I went round to her side of the table and asked if I might borrow her pen for a moment. She held it out at once. I took it and wrote a quick note. As I did so I became aware of her stare. Not the expected smile – she was giving me a really funny look, so much so that it was somewhat unnerving. As I finished writing and looked up at her I realised what was wrong: "You don't work here, do you?" I said, having seen her name badge up close. "No," she replied, "I work in the department store over there." She pointed vaguely over her shoulder and out beyond the glass wall dividing the shop from the arcades. I had certainly not intended to accost a fellow customer, even with so small a thing as requesting to use their pen, and felt I had to apologise. She then seemed to understand the situation – and my mistake – and smiled as I hurriedly handed her pen back. It was a nice smile too. Perhaps it could have been the start of a beautiful friendship. Perhaps the situation provides a new dating opportunity, at least for any younger, unattached readers; a coffee shop was only a few metres away. What an opportunity. After all we both browsed bookshops and wrote things down; maybe we read the same things too. But the moment had passed and we went on our separate ways, never to meet again. There was a silver lining, though. I bought yet another new book and loved it; that made me smile too.

*

Anything at all that will make some money seems to give rise to a business in Thailand, and anything new will, if it sells, rapidly be available everywhere. Tooth whitening is popular; medical services are much less expensive than in the countries that most tourists come from and they are good too. You cannot just get your teeth whitened with confidence, but have your appendix removed or your hip replaced, assured that the smiling medics know what they are doing. Perhaps with something like hips, if there is any language gap, you should concentrate firmly on the Thai words for left and right.

Some things offered are much more frivolous. A new one that seemed to appear suddenly and spread rapidly, perhaps because it must be so low cost to supply, is the fish pedicure. Originating in Japan, this takes the form of the customer removing their shoes and socks and sitting with their feet immersed in a tank of water reaching half way up their calves. In the tank, fish – some two, three inches long – nibble off all the dead skin and your feet emerge pristine and rejuvenated. It is not really cheap; I have seen it priced at *baht* 250 (about five pounds sterling) for 15 minutes, yet many people appear to give it a go. The fish – what is used is a kind of carp, the garra rufa, sometimes known as "Doctor fish" – are fed little or nothing else so they go to their work with a vengeance. Despite being toothless, after 15 minutes there is not a callus in sight. I am not sure it's for me. What if they were not so hungry or are messy eaters and my feet were being washed with a dilute solution containing assorted fragments of the last customers' dead skin? What if they get their fish muddled up with the kind of fighting fish that are used to encourage betting in some bars; or the odd stray piranha? I don't fancy that, and even more I don't fancy the sheer boredom of the exercise. The tickling sensation might distract for a moment, but I would need a good book, and one sign I saw did make me smile. It said: Customers are limited to 1½ hours. This seems incredible. What kind of state would your feet need to be in for someone to go for that and, if 15 minutes proved less than engaging, what would you do for a full hour and half? This would not just need a good book; it would need a copy of something like *War and Peace*, a couple of sandwiches and an iPod. Nevertheless, as I write this there are people sitting in little rows around tanks all over Thailand, apparently enjoying it very much. Whatever tickles your fancy, I suppose, or in this case your feet. And as I heard one wag say about the business prospects for the operators, who incidentally have to do little more than collect the money, "Fins are looking up". Since I wrote this it has appeared literally around the world and you can probably give it a go in your local high street; but only in Thailand I suspect is the service offered with shouts of "Some feeting for you".

*

I was once run off the road and left stranded by a taxi driver faced with a monsoon storm. What a storm. We all hate it when it rains, but even England's famously despised weather on a wet day cannot compete with the rain in countries like Thailand when the monsoon period comes. The rain then is truly biblical in proportion. It may not last long, sometimes a downpour lasts only a few minutes, but to say it is heavy misrepresents it in a big way. I do not mean heavy in terms of weight. Elephants are heavy, as are my wife's suitcases – wherever we go and for however a brief time – and so too are most of the hamburger eaters in America, but here the word heavy describes the intensity as well as the weight of water. Often more rain bounces up off the pavements in Bangkok when it rains than usually falls down in many parts of the world with dryer climates.

In England it can rain all day; indeed, I once spent a damp and miserable week in Scotland when it did not stop raining at all for the full seven days and my children went from mere boredom to becoming virtually psychotic. Though I have memories of them climbing waterfalls in the rain and of my son water-skiing on a loch with more water above him than below, so we must have got out a bit. We all spend long periods putting up with and dealing with wet weather. We have waterproof coats and hats, we have Wellington boots and we have umbrellas. Every move during a wet day involves protecting ourselves from the wet, sheltering from it and drying off after we have failed to do that and got soaked anyway. Oh yes, and we moan about it endlessly, even in the occasional summers when the grass is brown and farmers throughout the country are tearing their hair out.

Chapter Twelve

In Thailand, the attitude to rain seems radically different from that which I experience, and share, at home. There is a tacit acceptance of the seasons and of the rain they bring. It is a green and verdant country, agriculture thrives, rice is exported in large quantities and it is not much of an exaggeration to say that anything that you stick in the ground grows... and grows, and grows quickly. The reason is that there is enough rain, coupled with the high temperatures, to make this so. So, first off people want the rain, they know the crops want it, gardens and plants want it, and it is welcome also because it takes the heat and humidity out of the air to some extent, at least for a while.

Secondly, people don't seem to find it inconvenient, or at least not something to make a great song and dance about if they do. Of course, traffic slows when it rains, but then if there is anything in Bangkok that people are well used to it is slow traffic. It is just another excuse for being late to meet someone. Punctuality is hardly a high-ranking Thai virtue; as Siripan once said to me after I had waited for her for the best part of an hour, "I'm not late. I'm on time – my time". Indeed, in many people punctuality is hardly noticeable as a trait at all so, when it rains, for the most part people just stay put. In a café they look out the window and order another coffee. Outside a café, they go in and order a drink, pausing only to buy a newspaper on the way. "Wait it out" seems a common reaction. While raincoats and other such paraphernalia may be rare or non-existent – there is a small selection of rainwear and warm clothing in some stores for those travelling to colder countries – some people do carry umbrellas, usually small folding ones. Thus if someone has to rush out in the rain they do so with the umbrella up, or a folded newspaper over their heads, and get a bit wet in the process, as much from the rickety nature of much street architecture as anything else. Many buildings have overhangs or awnings, and all seem to leak; guttering is a rarity. The drips and, in some cases, cascades that come down from all this can be as much of a hazard as the rain itself. The other difference here is the heat: get a bit wet and once you are under cover you dry off in just a few minutes. No great problem, it seems.

Even in situations where work must go on, rain is tolerated and life just goes on. Take a market: at the threat of rain, and usually the sky blackens and all the signs are there ahead of any precipitation, plastic sheeting is deployed to cover the stalls and the walkways between. Each stallholder seems to deal with matters in their own vicinity. This means that the sheets are of different weights and colours: a veritable jigsaw of plastic is hastily clipped together, office style bulldog clips are often the method of choice to do so, and the rain is thus kept at bay. But such an ad hoc solution is far from perfect. There are gaps, there are drips and there are sagging areas of plastic that fill with water which, of course, are then apt to burst – sending a momentary deluge onto those below them. Again, all this is recovered from with little hassle; I even once saw a sizable awning collapse under the weight of water it had collected and drench a New Year's Eve spread being held in a hotel garden. For a few moments there was some consternation, but in minutes, seemingly, the staff swung into action, repairs were made, tables were laid again and the party continued as before.

Back to my being stranded: at the airport I once shared a taxi into town with another Englishman. The distinguished

Chapter Twelve

looking fellow was attending a military conference of some sort, probably seeking international collaboration to invade some errant state or other, but he had, it seemed, never been to the east before. As we proceded, the skies opened, rain deluged down and multiple forks of lightning rushed to earth and lit the sky ahead. Almost at once the taxi driver started to shake, his driving became erratic and eventually he slowed, nosed into the vegetation at the side of the road and refused to say a word. I turned to my military travelling companion, but far from coming up with an action plan he just looked totally miserable and kept muttering, "What do we do? What do we do?" I feared for Britain's military security, but it seemed we had no option but to get ourselves alternative transport. And so, given his inaction, I found myself out in the deluge trying to flag down another taxi, which to my surprise I did pretty promptly, though after even a brief spell at the side of the road I was way beyond soaked to the skin.

The second taxi duly took our suitcases aboard, completed the journey and I eventually walked into my hotel, looking a little less than smart hardly describes it; I left what looked like a small river behind me as I walked across the reception area. Checked in, in my room I had a hot shower and got changed. The rain had stopped by the time I looked out of my window. Despite my appearance and the ink smudges that appeared on my registration card as water ran down my sleeve as I signed in, nothing was said during my check in. It was raining – hard – and here that's normal enough.

No one seems to dwell on these things. If it rains it rains; *mai pen rai*. It takes more than a shower to wipe out smiles in this lovely country.

Chapter Thirteen

MAKING TRACKS

If God had intended us to fly
He would never have given us the railways.
Michael Flanders

The range of things that can be done in Thailand is staggering. Sightseeing can take you to sights such as the Grand Palace, a whole area of golden buildings, all impressive; the Royal barges housed nearby; a plethora of temples and Buddha images such as *Wat Arun*, which towers above the river and is a good place from which to get a great view or to see Japanese tourists descend en mass to noisily photograph each other. On the mainland or on countless islands you can go to the beach, to the country, the mountains and, if you wish you can be energetic, this is a place where you can go white water rafting, trekking, ride horses or elephants, snorkel and scuba dive and much more. Or you can watch go-go dancers, drink beer, have a traditional massage or, should you prefer, a less traditional massage. "Body massage" here may not mean that they massage your body, though they do, but may well mean that they use their body to massage yours. I am told that intimate hardly begins to describe such an experience. The realms of possibility are almost endless, but as I have said before the aim here is not to be a guidebook, but rather to give a flavour of visiting this special country. In this chapter, let me

Chapter Thirteen

introduce you to a minority activity – minority in the sense of being a special, and thus expensive, treat.

Sometimes when you look back, you marvel and wonder how something could possibly have happened just the way it did. A while ago I had what I thought was a good idea for a travel book: comparing travelling on a budget with a first class trip. I wrote up something about the idea, selecting as the core of the trip the Orient-Express type train – the Eastern & Oriental – that runs between Singapore, through Malaysia and into Thailand. I sent it to various publishers, all of whom either failed to reply or said a brief no thank you.

But I thought it was a good idea and I was persistent. It is said that there is one word that can be used to describe a writer who is not persistent. It's "unpublished". Remembering Henry Ford's sensible advice – "Failure is an opportunity to start again, more intelligently" – I added to the idea a bit, completely ignoring the "intelligently" aspect of said advice, for instance saying that the book would be amusing, and neglecting to realise that this would make it more difficult to write. Eventually, as I followed up my approaches, one company did reply, sending me an email saying "I don't remember this". Not very promising, but they did add a request to send it again, which I did. Within a few days a reply came saying something like "Of course I remember it, my boss has been looking at it and there's a contract in the post".

It is the nature of such moments that you move in a split second from many months of fussing over an idea to having an actual contract, a project and, not least, a deadline. And, in this case, a headache. Something else I had overlooked was the cost of making the trip; I was clearly going to need to sell a million copies just to break even. So, I began by writing begging letters to airlines, hotels and others in an attempt to get the cost down, while firmly avoiding promising that I would write nice things about them in case anything went wrong and I wanted to point that out. Various deals were struck. The airline upgraded me on a planned and booked flight and some of the recipients of my missives welcomed me with open arms, including Raffles in Singapore, the ultimate first class emporium from which I hoped to be able start the journey. Phew: the project was underway.

I made the booking, bought a smart new notebook, and created a new file on the computer.

The trip was difficult enough to make into an economic project for me alone, so in my enthusiasm for the work I arranged to travel solo, leaving my wife at home. I ignored her thoughts on it being something we could do together, repeating like a mantra, "It's just work, it's just work". I am not sure how this happened, how I got her to agree, but she did (thank you, dear) and the result was my book, *First Class At Last!*. To be fair, and before you write me off as an unfeeling brute, the book would probably not have happened otherwise and besides, we did another special trip about a year later – together (and this resulted in my book, *Beguiling Burma)*.

Why am I telling you all this? Because, while I was engaged in writing this book, it occurred to me that the train should make an appearance again. A train ride is, after all, a wonderful way to see a country. I didn't want to repeat the original experience (not least because the topic here is Thailand), so I made arrangements to make the journey north, the route having recently been extended to the north

Chapter Thirteen

of Bangkok since my first trip. You will not be surprised to hear that this time my wife came too. I may be keen on my writing activities, but I definitely don't have a death wish. In due course we abandoned the beach and set off for Bangkok and for The Oriental Hotel, at which intending passengers were to assemble to be taken to the station. Where else? A posh ride deserves a posh starting point.

*

Trains can be a good way to travel, but they are assuredly not all posh. Trains do have what can undoubtedly be described as a mixed image. Ask a commuter, struggling into London or some other city on a grubby train, without a seat, with arrival time varying day by day, and paying substantial and increasing amounts of money year by year for the privilege, and you will not get a flattering account. Train company officials are often thought to rank with estate agents and, more recently, bankers as at best candidates for the stocks. In the U.K., rail services have deteriorated over the years. When I bought my first house, the choice of location was heavily influenced by tracking various train lines out of London until I reached an area where I could afford to buy something; commuting was simply a necessity. Mind you, it was also quite a civilised process. You always got a seat; on my very first journey I remember being asked by a fellow passenger – very politely – if I would mind moving as I was sitting in the regular seat of another passenger due to join the train at the next station.

The country station where I started and finished my early journeys was tiny and the main member of staff, Harry, was chatty and welcoming to all. It was a somewhat leisurely business, too. Harry took his time, but everything seemed to get done – even if, as a friend reported to me, he once told someone that "If I go any slower I'll be in reverse". His character was defined for me when I once drove past the level crossing at the station late at night. Rather oddly, one gate was open, the other closed. I waited, then I sounded the horn, and Harry appeared to open the one closed gate. As I drove across, I opened the car window and asked him why the gates had been set as they were. "Well, to tell you the truth," he said apparently in all seriousness, "I'm half expecting a train." I saw him in the mirror carefully reclosing the one gate after I had passed.

Nowadays, there are certainly some good trains. I love the train through the channel tunnel, for instance; it's good, and anything that avoids the average airport experience makes good sense. Others provide a unique experience. I have once or twice travelled on trains in India and will always remember going north from Mumbai to a Hill Station for a break from the city: the sights and sounds along the way, including perhaps the most spectacular sunset I have ever seen, were wonderful. The downside there is the poverty and it was upsetting to see people living in tiny shacks just feet from the tracks. When I commented on this at the hotel I got what I have always regarded a very insightful answer: "Don't be mistaken, India is not a very poor country, it is a very rich country; it just happens to have a great many poor people too." In effect, it is a country where two populations share the same geographic space.

So, there are trains and trains, but the Orient Express and its cousin the South East Asian equivalent, the Eastern & Oriental train, are in a class of their own. Commuting this is not. The Orient Express defines the word "iconic". The company operate many hotels and resorts around the world, but it is the train everyone associates with the name. It conjures up pictures of old time luxury and dates back to a period when rail travel was the only way to see the world. Travel by rail is, I have always thought, an excellent way to see the countryside; the views are there all the time and so too is someone to look after you. The service on this train has been renown since 1883, when the first trip went from Paris to Istanbul. Today, some of Europe's greatest cities are on its route and provide sights for passengers as it pauses on its journeys. Since its early days it has come to be regarded as one of *the* great travel experiences and, more recently, the Eastern & Oriental train, which wends its way along the South East Asian peninsula northwards from Singapore through Malaysia and into Thailand, has acquired a similar reputation. It is run not just as a journey but as an experience and a way of engaging with the sights and sounds along the way. A new route north from Bangkok has been added only recently and it was this we were to experience. So, to the Oriental Hotel: though we were to discover that the start was not to go quite to plan.

*

The train was late.

We had a note, a very polite note, to say so. The delay got longer and another note evidently arrived at our hotel in Hua Hin – half an hour after we had left to travel to Bangkok to join the train. Being British I am well used to trains being late. This occurs with depressing regularity. In winter there are leaves on the line, signalling problems, engineering work – a term I am convinced means that very little is happening except that half the line is closed and buses are laid on to bridge the gap; they are usually late too. Or a couple of snowflakes fall and, needless to say, it may be very little, but it is inevitably the wrong kind of snow and everything grinds to a halt. In summer, of course, the weather is not much better; actually, let's be fair, we do have an English summer, usually in July, on a Tuesday... in the afternoon. But other hazards occur then, too, particularly staff shortages and strikes.

Neither of the polite notes gave a reason for the delay, just saying the train was late in arriving from Singapore and that there was a "Temporary track closure in Southern Thailand". Why not say why? It transpired that flash floods after an unexpected torrential storm at the border between Malaysia and Thailand had swept away some track. I am used to poor excuses, but this was surely a perfectly good one; even the most curmudgeonly traveller could not expect a train to proceed without rails. It further transpired that attempts to get this fixed had proved difficult as requests for repair had been greeted by the response, "No way, governor, not until after Chinese New Year", or with words to that effect. Chinese New Year is an extended holiday, but despite this the worthy officials of Eastern & Oriental had somehow got things moving – passengers on the train were disembarked and flown back to Singapore, the railway authorities were somehow prevailed upon to make the necessary repair and being just a few hours late was really very good in the circumstances.

We arrived at the Oriental Hotel well ahead of the actual departure, but where better to wait than in such an august establishment? In due course, the staff from the train checked us in, whisked our luggage away and treated us to dinner at the Oriental's famous riverside buffet. Very nice it was too. I was able to have a nice cold *Singha* beer, but there was no tonic water, an odd omission that turned out to be not an oversight of the hotel but evidence of the floods that had damaged Bangkok only a few months earlier. The factory had been flooded and was still working below capacity. The only real blot on the arrangements was when tea was served earlier in the hotel function room used for check-in and, somehow, the staff at the Oriental – a hotel as famous for its afternoon tea taken in the beautiful Authors' Lounge, as anything else – managed to make it with cold water. When this was pointed out, the server rushed away apologising and promising to rectify the matter "at once". She returned 10 minutes later with fresh tea – also stone cold. Someone was surely having a bad day.

Initially, several passengers complained about the delay. We were, after all, missing some hours on the train and should have been looking out over the lush Thai countryside, but when the circumstances were explained most accepted the situation. Indeed, when I checked again with the train manager at the end of the journey, matters appeared to have been made up sufficiently well for all grumblings to have been washed away in a sea of satisfaction. This is an iconic train and the journey proved to be just wonderful. It was a spoil with a capital S.

After dinner on the terrace, we were soon delivered to Hualumpong Station, quite a small scale establishment for a big city, where the train, 21 coaches long, stretched into the distance along the platform. The whole length was smartly painted in the E & O's distinctive green and cream livery. It was easier to walk along the platform than it was later to walk through the train corridor, which needs careful navigation when the train is moving and can easily cause bruises as you bang the sides. The gauge of the, mainly single, track is narrower than in Europe and this exaggerates the movement. We were quickly on board the train, unpacking and settling in for the night in our designated compartment; our luggage was already waiting for us when we got there. Our carriage steward, Thamasin, who had also looked after me on my previous journey, briefed us about the cabin and arranged to deliver our breakfast in the morning, breakfast being a bit-more-than-continental served on a tray: rolls, croissants, fruit and fruit juice, cereal, yogurt and tea or coffee.

Next we spent some interesting time circling each other like animals marking out their territory. If I moved a bit *this* way, and my wife moved a bit *that* way, we could get ourselves organised. I had forgotten just how small the compartments were; furthermore I had been on my own on the last trip so had twice as much space. It took a moment. When I moved *this* way and she moved *that*, the train moved another way and threw our calculations out completely. I imagined this dance being enacted up and down the train; all those sharing a compartment needed to be good friends. Despite the small size, the compartments are a wonder of careful design which just work and there is room to exist comfortably in them; one of the beds disappears into the wall during the day and provides additional space. With their stunning décor of cherry wood, they also combine a feeling of the luxurious with the exotic. This really is a very special way to travel.

Chapter Thirteen

In the morning someone asked me, "Did you have a good sleep?" and I answered "Yes, several", because the motion of the train had me stirring a number of times but then falling asleep again in what were narrow but perfectly comfortable beds. My wife slept less well, but it was her first time aboard and besides she is the ultimate insomniac; when I wake in the morning at home I never know whether she is about to wake too, or is just getting settled. I creep away, often discovering notes around the house as testament to her nocturnal activities: "Hi, I was just thinking about... can you...?" Some reported taking anti-travel sickness pills or sleeping tablets at first, but all the passengers said they got used to the motion as the trip passed. For my part, by the third night I hardly stirred.

We were awake quite early and the scenes going by were fascinating. As the sun rose the countryside rolled by: rice fields, sugar cane, rivers, lakes, open country and some signs of habitation – some buildings, small villages and a few isolated people. I saw one solitary man washing in a stream apparently miles from anywhere. Elsewhere, a market was being set up and, on one occasion, we stopped momentarily alongside a train going the other way, its passengers staring curiously at us out of open carriages bereft of air conditioning or any other kind of comfort. Never mind, normal trains span the country and are well liked and much used. We passed several small stations, each little more than a platform and a tiny building: one, Tha Chang, had a 12-foot statue of an elephant on the platform; I'm not sure if it was there to greet passengers or if it was waiting for a train. All station staff, even in small stations, are well turned out and wear almost military style uniforms. There is some pomp and ceremony involved in such jobs; in Hua Hin, for instance, train arrivals are announced by ringing an ancient and highly polished brass bell – just because it's a nice thing to do.

Once we were up and about, we began to meet our fellow passengers. The train has public areas consisting of three dining cars, a bar/lounge, a reading room and an open air observation car. On this trip, the passengers came from 17 different countries, which was something of a record, as Leesa Lovelace, the E & O General Manager from Singapore, told us later. There were some nice people. Some were clearly of very considerable means and talk touched regularly on other trips and destinations, all taken in style. Often three or four trips were mentioned and it became clear that this was just where someone had been in the last year. We only managed to keep up in any way by invoking a lifetime's travel; I mentioned Buenos Aires to one fellow passenger even though I had been there but once, on a business trip when I spoke at a conference. Another sign of the kind of people taking the trip was that enquiries about where someone lived were regularly answered with a list. One fellow passenger told us they had homes in Sydney, Melbourne and Hong Kong, but that visiting London had been a bit of a problem since they sold the house in Kensington. Kensington: a London borough which probably has one of the highest property values in the U.K. Others were less overt about their circumstances and some were only aboard as a special treat; one British couple living in Singapore, and with as far as I know only one house, had been given their trip as a present from their son so that they could celebrate a special anniversary.

Chapter Thirteen

We also met more of the staff who would serve us during the journey. Leesa Lovelace was to travel with the train during this whole journey, something she did about once a month to keep close to the operation and its passengers. As 60 percent of the staff has worked on the train ever since it started operating in 1991, some of the faces, like Thamasin our steward, were familiar to me from my earlier trip. One of those was Nuchjaree who runs the bar carriage. I remember being quizzed by my wife when I wrote about her in my earlier book, saying that "She combined her beauty with an air of quiet competence, but this did nothing to dilute the beauty. She was simply drop-everything, leave home and start a new life beautiful." I It was true and, I thought, rather well put. She recognised me at once and greeted me not just by telling me that she had read my book "... most of it and all of what it said about me. I like it", but also quoted some of it to me verbatim. I promised to mention her again here and say something different about her. But let me say that I don't think my earlier description can be bettered and, to be business-like for a moment, the service in her domain was second to none. Forget the train and the sights, I would travel again just to see her... but my wife will read this so let's leave it there.

Also aboard was Else Geraets, an expert on textiles and there to talk us through one of our excursions. She had started by saying a few words at the Oriental Hotel and her knowledge and experience was quickly demonstrated. A tall woman with short grey hair, she was a volunteer worker at the Thai National Museum and had lived around Asia for many years. She was also elegance personified: her slim figure appearing regularly throughout the trip and she was seemingly dressed in a different outfit each time. Certainly she was wearing a different woven scarf every time I saw her, and explained that Laos's textiles were probably superior to those made in Thailand. Wherever hers originated, they looked truly beautiful.

The train stops to allow passengers to undertake various excursions and on one of these we saw a demonstration of weaving and learnt that the kind pattern that Else favoured was created at the work rate of about six or seven centimetres per day. That's slower than some glaciers. The way it was done was intriguing. First a template was made of the design, then shuttles went to and fro and a bewildering array of fine silk threads were organised with a dexterity that seemed like witchcraft. It was all done by women, mothers teaching daughters, and it was a delight to see such a traditional skill thriving. The hand-made nature of such fabric made it comparatively expensive. The studio we visited had just completed one order for a New Yorker consisting of 220 metres of fabric! It took two and a half years to complete the order and necessitated, as the owner put it, "a considerable amount of money being paid up front". Very wise.

The first of these excursions was to a temple. We all trooped into buses and we found ourselves in Bus 1, under the care and guidance of "Patti". Her real name was lengthy and nicknames are common here, at least *farang* are often offered one to use – "to say easier". We were now some 200 miles north of Bangkok and she told us about the area we were in, *Phi Mai*, and also offered various sundry facts, for instance about bananas. In Thailand fruit is plentiful and wonderful. Bananas not only come looking very like those we eat in England, but also in a miniature variety, just three or four inches long. These, she explained, are called monkey bananas

Chapter Thirteen

because they form the treat fed to monkeys to train them to climb trees and harvest coconuts. Now how have I survived so many visits to Thailand without ever knowing that?

Our destination was in Phimai Historical Park: it was Prasat Hin Phimai, one of the most important Mahayana Buddhist temples in Thailand. This was built sometime over the 11th/12th centuries and was then the centrepiece of an ancient town. The temple is in ruins, though the Department of Fine Arts is making some restorations; it is still impressive and what is there makes it easy to imagine the whole, with its red sandstone walls, towers and decorations pristine. The decorative carvings depict Buddhist themes, though those from the earliest period of its existence have Hindu origins. It dates back to the Khmer kingdom and in style it mirrors the well-known Cambodian temple at Angkor – Angkor Wat. It is, in fact, believed that it influenced the design of the better known Angkor Wat. We had time to wander through its various "layers", going from outer walls into an inner temple topped by three towers and entered through a series of narrow passages.

Nothing on this trip was just a visit. Here, a troupe of dancers, colourfully dressed men and women, welcomed us and performed again as we ended our visit and moved back to the buses.

In a hot country sightseeing makes you thirsty.

Wine has not been much drunk in Thailand in the past. It is expensive and the journey to Thailand from the main wine-producing countries does it no great favours. However, this is changing. Many tourists, used to a glass or two of wine at home, want it and more and more locals are acquiring the habit too. So it is increasingly more in evidence. Very recently there has been another development: wine is being produced in Thailand. Not just any old wine either, by all accounts, but some that is really well regarded. Near the train route, in Khao Yai National Park, a beautiful mountain region, is Granmonte, a winery famous for being run by the first woman winemaker in Thailand.

We went to visit.

Our buses pulled up outside an attractive low-rise building containing a shop, a restaurant – "VinCotto" – and an outdoor seating area for tasting sessions; fields of vines surrounded it with mountain views beyond. The vines have been chosen to flourish in tropical climes and produce what are called "New Latitude Wines". We were welcomed by the owner, who quickly took a back seat after introducing us to his daughter "Nikki", the first woman winemaker and still in her 20s, I would have thought, though she had found time to train in a winery in Adelaide's famous Barossa valley, in South Australia. And in Portugal... and in France; she seemed well qualified and told us how her father had set up the winery "because he likes to drink it and wanted a hobby", and how she was in charge of the vines, the harvesting, the winemaking and just about everything, really. She ended her introduction by saying that her father "sometimes helped" and that all financial matters were firmly in the hands of her mother. A ripple of approval went round the women in the group at this last comment and her mother smiled a you-had-better-believe-it smile from the sidelines. Her husband nodded. He appeared to believe his hobby was in good hands.

Granmonte now produces 120,000 bottles of wine each year, red, white and rose, from some 50 acres of vines. They even export some, 20 percent of their production in fact, and to countries including winemaker Germany: no mean achievement. "Nikki" told us that the winery had won many awards, adding modestly – but powerfully – "too many to list". We all looked suitably impressed. All this was the result of some considerable investment. The actual production building was a spotless wonder of stainless steel: huge vats ranged around the actual winery building together with machines to take care of everything, from stripping the grapes from the vines to bottling the final product. But what did it taste like?

Well, as someone who does not drink wine I have no idea, though I can report that the cheese that was provided to go with the tasting was delicious. I sipped iced water, having decided that asking for a beer at a wine tasting was probably just not done; though given the hospitality lavished on us I suspect I would have been served an icy glass in a moment. Looking round I saw that the rest of the group clearly rated it highly. Five wines were supplied for tasting; all were pronounced good. Did I detect that the final one was easier to lavish praise on just because it had been preceded by four other glasses? Was that someone saying "shhupeerb"? Surely not! Actually, a number of those present, those in the group who seemingly really knew their wines, did rate it highly. All those awards seem to have been justified. It made a pleasant visit. It also showed a Thai business woman in a very positive light. "Nikki" knew her stuff. Dressed in jeans and heavy boots she looked the part, was attractive and confident, and she described their work with passion, a sense of humour, in a way that showed she loved what she was doing and thought it was special. She smiled as she sent us on her way. If you like your wines and see the label Granmonte, it may just be worth a try; a wine from the land of smiles should be pleasant to drink.

Regularly, as the journey progressed, neat invitation cards appeared in each compartment telling passengers in which dining car, and at which table, they would take the next meal. We were mixed, rotated and moved about. I wondered how this was done and later was shown the chart the chief steward, actually called the Maitre d'Hotel, compiled ahead of each meal: he took into account various criteria: nationality, language – having people unable to speak to each other would not add to the spirit of the occasion – and an alchemy of other factors about which he remained firmly secretive. It was a painstaking process, one based partly on observation and one that also had to accommodate passenger preference: that is, those that wanted to be alone, some tables just for two, those who wanted to sit with friends, new or otherwise, or indeed avoid someone – *just make sure I never sit with that bore again.* However it was done, it made for interesting meal times.

Given that I was to write something about the trip, it was no surprise to find we had dinner one night with Leesa Lovelace. She had been with the company for 17 years, two fewer than the train's manager, Ulf Buchert, both providing more evidence of the way that staff stick with the train. She told me something about the staffing of the train. At the start it had been the intention for staff to represent the overall route, with people from Singapore, Malaysia and Thailand. But the job is taxing and quite quickly it appeared that the Thais were best suited for the job. Now almost every member of the team is Thai, with just a few of those in the kitchens being the exception. Leesa explained that at first the Thais

Chapter Thirteen

had been somewhat reserved. They were excellent at providing the service required, but reluctant, perhaps embarrassed, to speak to passengers in a way that did more than just respond. "We needed them to engage with people," said Leesa. They worked at it, and gradually recruitment and training achieved the style and excellence seen today. The key was teamwork. People had to get on together and, when I asked Ulf Buchert how it was he had stayed so long, this is what he stressed. Beyond simply being involved in such a travel icon, it was the team that kept him there: "It is not just a team," he said, "it's a family."

Before and after the meals the bar in the lounge car was open; in fact, on this particular trip, drinks from beverages to beer, were all complimentary. This was another mixing area as people sat in the long narrow area and fell into conversation with their fellow passengers. In the evening, the train's pianist, an elderly Chinese from Singapore, was in attendance. No one seemed to over indulge, unless they did so after my bedtime, though the pianist recounted how he had got his job because the previous incumbent, unable to resist the drinks given to him by passengers, regularly became rather wobbly in his playing and a replacement was called for. Music added to the occasion and on the last evening a Thai dancer preformed before dinner. Thai dancing is a magical mix of precision and motion. She was colourfully dressed and wore long extensions to her fingers to enhance the characteristic hand movements that are always evident in Thai dancing. With the bar centrally placed, she repeated her dance at either end of the car so that everyone could see. Charming, and almost as graceful as Nuchjaree pouring me a cup of tea with complete precision even as the train rattled over some points.

Smile Because It Happened

On this last evening, passengers are requested to dress not just smartly, but more formally: that means a jacket and tie for the men. With an eye on service and customer relations there is no actual instruction and I do not think you would be refused dinner for appearing tie-less (on this trip nobody did), but the request was polite but firm. It seemed to imply that transgression would be letting the side down and reminded me of an old boss of mine who had a favourite phrase and was wont to say, "It's only a suggestion, but do bear in mind who's making it". In the event, everyone looked very smart and the occasion benefited. One other "instruction" was followed by most passengers. When we had watched the weaving, we were also able to create a silk scarf, not one woven at seven inches a day, but one patterned and dyed. In the evening they had been finished and delivered back to our compartments to be worn at dinner – "No scarf, no drink" was the mantra.

Service is a fragile flower. Bad service is instantly recognisable and resented. Even generally high standards can easily be let down, witness the story of an American hotel magnate staying in one of his own properties. He was not impressed and matters came to a head at breakfast. He introduced himself to his waitress and said, expressing his dissatisfaction, "We need to give all our customers three things: good food, a pleasant word and a nice smile." She nodded vigorously and was sent to get him some scrambled eggs and bacon. It arrived promptly. He looked at her and waited and was rewarded by a thin smile. "And a pleasant word?" he queried. Without hesitation she replied, "I recommend you don't eat the eggs." True or not, it makes a good point about the fragility of service.

Chapter Thirteen

Service must be efficient, yet it is nice if it is friendly too. If it is too friendly, however, it can quickly seem intrusive and inappropriate or, at worst, insincere and annoying. I don't think I have ever seen a better blend of service excellence and friendliness than that exhibited by the staff on this extraordinary train. For my money, they get it just exactly right. They can serve a meal with care and precision, and neither silverware, classic china or anything else you would think a moving train might make difficult phases them. They also create a friendly, informal atmosphere amongst their passengers, yet at the same time nothing is too much trouble. If you want some information – or just a chat – then that is provided too, happily and with a smile. The meals themselves must get 10 out of 10 for both the dishes served and the presentation, so full marks to all those who are involved in their preparation.

All the staff aboard appear to love their jobs, which says something about both the quality of those employed and how they are managed. Leesa explained that there are rarely vacancies and if there is, it can almost always be filled informally: one or other of the existing people will know someone suitable who wants to join the team. I am sure that is so.

The last port of call before we set off back towards Bangkok, took us into Laos. We crossed the river Mekong on the Friendship Bridge, funded and built by Australians, and opened in 1994 to provide a modern crossing for both traffic and trains as well as pedestrians.

Laos is a comparatively small and landlocked country, with a population of around six or seven million people. It may have nothing to do with the size of the population, but I noticed that this is a country that allows *mia nois,* or minor wives. This is not an idea that finds favour in many places these dayse We had come aboard with passport photos ready and forms completed and someone aboard was charged with obtaining visas for every passenger. With typical E & O efficiency, our passports were simply collected a little ahead of the border crossing and quietly returned later. No fuss, no hassle: job done. The core of our time in Laos involved a stop in the capital, Vientiane. Because we are here focused on Thailand I will not go into detail about this trip, other than to say it was an interesting part of the overall journey.

Two things, however, I will make an exception for. On departing from the train we sat at the front of Bus 1 and ahead of us a police motor bike was parked. As we set off, two policemen mounted the bike and it became clear that they were an escort for us. The bus pulled away on the right hand side of the road, a bit odd as in Thailand they drive on the left (as they do on the bridge) – a legacy of the fact that the first car imported into Thailand (by the King) was brought from England. A blue light flashed on a stalk at the rear of the bike, occasional bursts of a siren alerted traffic to our presence and succeeded in making it part in front of us. The policeman on the back of the bike waved both arms in an elaborate dance, first fending off a car, then another bike or a truck. Occasionally, when a response was slow in coming, he became extra animated, the driver zoomed to and fro alongside and ahead of the offending motorist who quickly pulled over. They even had to wave at oncoming traffic which occasionally seemed to drift into the middle of the road and thus risk us having to slow. It was quite an experience and certainly a solution for any commuter frustrated by their journey to work,

Chapter Thirteen

albeit a difficult one to arrange. However, it seemed E & O could arrange almost anything.

The second thing that caught my attention and which does have a bearing on Thailand was a story told to us about the Emerald Buddha, a statue that was captured by Thais and taken to Thailand in some long ago skirmish. Evidently it has always been prophesied that the time would come for its return and that if that moment was missed then misfortune would befall the Thai nation. This was mentioned because just a few months previously Thailand had suffered major flooding. The statue remained unreturned and what was the main misfortune predicted in such circumstances? It was flooding. I am not superstitious, but given how much of the country and a major part of Bangkok was inundated, it might just be worth returning it to its original home; would Thailand of all countries miss just one Buddha image?

Because the train was running a little late still, as we approached Bangkok it made an extra stop to let off two people who were in some danger of missing a flight to Singapore, one a lady who had amused us by saying that she and her husband lived in different countries: "A good arrangement," she said. A stop was found alongside the expressway where a taxi was ready and waiting, they were whisked on their way and should have checked in successfully in time to meet their departure deadline; all part of the service. Most of the rest of the passengers, ourselves included, were happy to have a little longer after rising to watch the last of the scenery through the windows as we headed for Bangkok. The last stretch showed just how built up Bangkok is, a city of 10 million people, a proportion of whom live in simple and overcrowded conditions. The city is a magnet for people from up country hoping for a better life and is still growing in size. When the train stopped, we saw and thanked Thamasan and when we disembarked we found many of the staff lined up to wish us well on our way; I paused briefly as we went along the line, positioned at the front of the train, and promised Nuchjaree a sight of this chapter in due course. The trip ended, as it had begun, at the Oriental Hotel, where taking lunch needs a mortgage – though not, I suspect, for many of our fellow passengers. As this was not included as part of the arrangements, we ate elsewhere before our taxi arrived to take us back to Hua Hin. Travelling in style is hard work and we needed a few more days to recuperate by the beach to finish the trip.

And what about my wife – had our travelling together made up for my viewing the first train trip as work, even bearing in mind that it did result in my first travel book being published? Was I forgiven? It must be said that she enjoyed the trip enormously, as surely anyone would, so whilst I did not actually ask for forgiveness for the effect my earlier work had had on her, I think all is well on that front now. Looking ahead, if I have a yen to write about anywhere else that is essentially pleasant then I suspect that I will have to get two tickets.

*

After so much that is positive in this chapter, perhaps I should mention, just to balance things up and illustrate that travel can sometimes be a pig, that the trip that included the epic train journey ended at a time when significant snow

Chapter Thirteen

swept across Europe. We arrived at Bangkok airport at 11.00 in the morning and, after what seemed like a lifetime, did not take off until nearly 04.00 the next day. The flight added 12 hours, Heathrow got us off the plane and out of the airport with an indifference to time that even the Thais would be hard pressed to emulate, and when all of this was done, we received a text from the taxi driver due to meet us at the airport saying that he could not get the car out of his driveway. On finally arriving home by train, from which a kind neighbour collected us, we vowed never to travel again… until the next time.

In the many hours involved in waiting, I wrote a first draft of this chapter, read a whole book, walked what seemed like miles around the terminal, drank more cups of tea than I could count and found my body clock descending into an area of utter uncertainty in which I was not sure whether it was Tuesday or breakfast time. It is always nice to get home, however pleasant your travels have been, but on this occasion it was a palpable relief.

Enough gloom; it was a trip to remember. The world is full of places to visit and sights to see and it has an abundance of journeys to be made too, some hard, some less so. Travel by train can be a good way to explore and, at the luxury end of things, the Eastern & Oriental Express must rank high, very high. The experience it offers is great and the service is superb; together they create something very special. In my view the new northern route through Thailand is a worthy addition to the train's activities, though currently it is a less frequent part of their portfolio of journeys. It shows you parts of Thailand that are less well visited than the main tourist areas, and of course most of the staff who man the train are Thai. which extends your experience of the country and its people.

The theme here is smiles, so let's end comment about the train by returning to that. Did the journey make us smile? Everyone on this trip seemed to enjoy it enormously if the almost party spirit that built up during the journey was anything to go by. It certainly made me smile again. Perhaps the last word should go to the lovely Nuchjaree. As the train was drawing into Bangkok, someone commented that she must be pleased to be due a break. "That will make you smile," they said. "No need," she replied. "My job makes me smile." I'm sure that's true. And what she and the rest of the crew do and how they do it assuredly makes her passengers smile too. It is a classic case of smiles breeding more smiles.

Chapter Thirteen

Chapter Fourteen

AN ARRESTING EXPERIENCE

Policemen are numbered in case they get lost.
Spike Milligan

The beach has cropped up more than once here, quite rightly as almost any beach in Thailand will make you smile. So let me end with an incident on the beach which I believe illustrates much about what makes Thailand and Thai people such a delightful antidote to any melancholy.

There are in my opinion, some things in life of which one never, ever tires. These include the taste of chocolate the first sip of a cold beer on a hot day, the sound of my favourite jazz singer Stacy Kent's delightful and irresistible voice – and, more relevant here, the sound of the sea on a beach. Staying at Siripan's hotel we were right on the beach; the sound of the sea was ever present. It greeted us in the morning, gradually entering the consciousness as sleep slowly departed; it filled my mind during a first solitary walk along the beach before breakfast, when my mind is is still gradually coming to terms with a new day; and it remained there throughout the day, changing its sound to reflect the subtleties of the wind and the tide. It was somehow in the background, yet also in mind whatever else was going on. It engendered calm and seemed to prompt reflection; certainly it added to the general sense of laziness that is required for a good holiday.

Chapter Fourteen

It was this sound, as well as the sun, the sea and the view, that made regular walks with friends irresistible. These occurred at various times during the day, but never without someone suggesting that walking would balance out the constant round of food and drink. Fat chance! One would have had to spend substantial time hounded by the toughest sergeant major in the world, and even then the exercise would not begin to catch up with the indulgence. But some walking was doubtless better than none, and the walks were done less for the exercise than to take in the view and continue our conversations with a change of scene.

Today, an early turn along the beach showed a small change to the tranquil scene. A grey naval vessel was moored off shore in the distance and launches buzzed to and fro around it. All this was sufficiently far away that it prompted no great thought about why it should be so. Breakfast quickly put it in the background. Sitting under the trees, the sunshine filtering through the palms, we made a leisurely start to the day.

This morning, breakfast involved freshly squeezed orange juice, and pineapple so ripe and perfect that even an experienced botanist would have been at a loss to equate it with the so-called pineapples usually seen in Europe, sundry other dishes, numerous cups of tea or coffee and an hour and a half of leisurely conversation during which plans were hatched for the day. Perhaps "plans" overstates it just a tad; the stay was, after all, designed to be a few days of total relaxation. There was a view tentatively expressed that we ought to go into town, but this was quickly scotched by the majority view that this was a waste of good idling time.

Smile Because It Happened

After breakfast, we walked along the beach, in what was referred to as a burst of "power idling", this phrase having been coined after we had seen a couple power walking along the beach at a great rate, using hiking sticks apparently to speed their progress. The sea sparkled, the sun shone and the battleship, or whatever it was, remained visible off in the distance. After half an hour or so of leisurely walking, we passed by an area of considerable activity. Several launches came and went from the shore, and on the sand a party of uniformed men were spread unevenly between the sea and the top of the beach. On closer inspection, they were clearly of three kinds: police, soldiers and navy frogmen, though they were assembled in mixed groups, seemingly grateful for the chance to fraternise. We could clearly identify them by their uniforms, especially the frogmen. It was the wetsuits and enormous serrated knives strapped to their thighs that gave them away. In a country where the average height is a good bit less than the European norm, they hardly towered over you. Nevertheless, an impressive array of armaments made their general purpose clear, and explained the naval vessel out to sea, which was moored opposite the King's palace in the distance.

It is well known that policeman seem to get younger and younger as you get older. Here the nearest figure was a policeman who looked about 14 years old. Even the seemingly over-large pistol at his hip did not make him appear too daunting a figure, so one of us asked him what was going on. With a few words and many gestures he supplied the detail. One of the Royal Princesses was visiting friends with a summer home on the beach; those around us were her guards.

Chapter Fourteen

I have mentioned the importance of the Royal family in Thailand; Thais, who will always refer to *my* King, rather than using the word "the", hold them in great respect and the royal family have an important role in public life. What is more, you can be imprisoned for 15 years just for being rude about them (*about* them not *to* them, goodness knows what that would mean) – so in this light the guards constituted a modest presence. The Princess wanted a quiet visit to friends at a house on the beach, no fuss and everyone round about to watch her on her jet ski. No problem. Want a day on the beach? Call the navy. And call the police and the army as well. A soldier was now fronting the group closest to us. We asked politely – it is surprising how politeness comes naturally in the presence of a submachine gun – whether we could walk further down the beach, and were waved on. Broad smiles all round widened at a thank you given in Thai.

The walk continued, and about half an hour later we returned to the same spot en route back to base. A mid-morning break and a long cool drink had grown in priority as the walk had progressed and the sun had risen higher in the sky. A soldier approached us with his hand raised. Clearly we were expected to stop. We did. He held a submachine gun about three sizes too big for him which more than made up for his apparent youth and inexperience. Hesitantly, we enquired what went on. He smiled, groped carefully into what proved to be his limited English vocabulary and said, "My Princess on beach". Yes. Right. We looked around, but any Royal figure seemed too far away to spot. Nevertheless, we expressed delight. We smiled. But when we tried to walk on, he repeated his performance: smile, pause, and the same comment, "My

Smile Because It Happened

Princess on beach". We were clearly expected to wait. We asked for how long this royal expedition might delay us. His face indicated that he was again consulting his mental lexicon. "Two hours," he said. Well, what he *actually* said was "*About* two hours," which, given the substantial inexactitude of most time statements in the land of smiles, might well have meant till Tuesday week.

After a moment I was deputed to negotiate. "Why me?" I wondered, watching his gun rise slightly as I stepped forward. He repeated his one phrase, "My Princess on beach", and it seemed to me that his smile began to give out mixed messages. Just because he did not speak much English did not mean he was not unfaltering in his duty to keep the beach clear of foreign feet while his Princess gambled in the surf. Others from the military force came closer and I attempted to explain to one – perhaps an officer? – that we would prefer not to stand in the sun for an unspecified amount of time, and that surely a few *farang* clad in beachwear and clearly unarmed did not pose a major threat to the royal personage. He thought about this and extended his colleague's vocabulary by two more words: "My Princess on beach. You wait." We waited, and I explained again to one of the others our need for rest, shade and the comfort of our hotel.

This time he produced a radio. He began talking to someone who proved to be visible further down the beach, as the conversation began to include gestures. His colleague began to approach, bringing more armaments with him. A long conversation ensued between the new arrival and our original sentry. The sentry was certainly not limited in his vocabulary in Thai. They spoke at length. The conversation

Chapter Fourteen

went to and fro between the two of them. It became more animated. Clearly it involved us. It also involved much pointing and, given that they both held firearms, it was these that did most of the pointing.

Finally, a decision seemed to have been made. More soldiers were called to become involved and it was made clear that we should walk away from the sea and up the beach, a route that effectively took us further away from the hotel. The original sentry now led the group, and further enquiry only produced the same four-word mantra, "My Princess on beach". So, we walked to the top of the beach, noticing as we did so that additional soldiers had surrounded us; guns and knives glinted in the bright sun. The radio was chattering and a jeep drew up as we climbed up from the sand onto the grass beyond. Its driver appeared to be the recipient of the radio calls. Suddenly, it all seemed too clear: we were apparently under arrest – impounded for the duration of the Princess's beach party, or longer. It was only a few days until our flights back to Europe. What were Thai jails like? Did offences against royalty involve capital punishment? How do you contact the British Embassy?

Our four-worded friend spoke to the driver of the jeep; a long explanation – or instructions on the precise form of incarceration selected for us – seemed to be involved. The driver nodded in reply. The two glanced at each other, then at us. Then the driver smiled at us. He spoke English. "Please get in," he said. "He asked me drive you to your hotel. Where do you stay?" Not to prison, then. I mumbled the hotel's name, as thoughts of a diet of dry rice and cockroach sandwiches began to fade. As we climbed into the jeep, the original soldier smiled. Not true – in fact he beamed. "My Princess on beach," he said again, and his beam became broader. His mind was working overtime as he searched his vocabulary further. Finally he summoned two more words in English: "My Princess okay – you okay!" His beam broadened still more.

It all fell into place. He had succeeded in resolving a major dilemma. He could not allow us along the beach. His duty to protect the Princess, even from so unlikely a threat as us, was clearly overriding. But neither did he want to inconvenience us; every Thai national understands the national importance of tourism. His solution was to stop us from going along the beach, but to allow – indeed assist – our return to the hotel. It was typical Thai pragmatism. He was delighted at the resolution. I thanked him profusely. We all did. And he beamed some more. He waved to us as we drove off. He did so without putting his gun down, and the barrel swung to and fro; we waved back in less military style and clung onto the sides of the swaying jeep as it whisked us back to the hotel.

Not too many guests at the hotel got an armed military escort back from their mid-morning walk. We made the most of it, ensuring that the driver delivered us to the door, and maintaining an enigmatic silence about what had occurred. The rumours amongst fellow guests and staff grew nicely, assisted by our whispers and our dropping the occasional louder word, such as "arrest". A round of cold drinks was welcome indeed.

Our moment of concern over, we discussed the activities for the remainder of the day as we drank – and, after due but leisurely consideration, decided to walk in the other direction after lunch. The biggest trouble with power idling is not that it prompts brushes with local troops; it is that it seems to

Chapter Fourteen

require just one darned decision after another. Besides, the soldier's resolution to the problem was so very Thai and, like so much in the land of smiles, so welcome.

*

So, in my opinion, here is one great antidote to gloom. It may be more than 5000 miles away, but there is something about Thailand, its people, its culture, indeed most everything about it. Of course, it has its problems, not least political. It is hot, sometimes too hot, and when it rains it can seem like you are under a waterfall. But it seems so easily to make you smile, or more likely it puts you in a mood where a smile comes easily. It's worth the journey.

The descriptions here stem from a number of visits and thus from a number of journeys. Most often I have flown out on a "night flight"; that is one arriving in Bangkok early in the morning, meaning the best thing to do for much of its duration is to sleep. My travel kit always includes a sleeping tablet and I move the time on my watch forward when I get on the plane and go on from there. Waking up just as the plane is due to land and having a big breakfast in your hotel is, I find, a positive step to minimising jet lag.

On the homeward leg I usually take a "day flight"; that's one leaving in the middle of the day and arriving back in the United Kingdom in the early evening. This gets me home in the early evening with an hour or two to unpack and get to bed at a normal time, and again this suits me well. But such a flight is 12 tedious hours during which, if I want to minimise jet lag, I find the best thing is to stay awake so that when I do get home and go to bed I find it easy to get a normal full night's sleep. But by no means all travellers share my logic here, and among those that don't are airlines.

On the flight home, as soon as take off is successfully completed, passengers are served a full meal – what is this: lunch, dinner? – at what is then about seven or eight o'clock in the morning at home. Three hours later, at around ten in the morning U.K. time, half the cabin is usually asleep and all the window blinds have been shut (mine definitely stays open if I can make it). Yet it is a proven reducer of jet lag to have as much daylight or bright light at the right times of day as possible. I read, work, even watch a dire film, but I aim to stay awake and I resolutely go by U.K. time during the flight, especially in terms of eating which, given the way the airlines operate, means I must bring appropriate snacks with me. Whichever stewardess looks after my seat area finds herself delivering regular cups of tea to me and they always seem at a loss to make out my eating habits, even when I decline the second full meal – what is referred to as "dinner" and served at four in the afternoon – they are still pressing me to join in with their perverse sense of timekeeping. On Thai Airways, incidentally, they do so in a delightful way. The air crew are smartly turned out, the women in outfits of Thai silk that tie in with elements of their national image and culture.

If there is any logic to how airlines arrange their timings, then it totally escapes me. Surely all logic suggests adopting the time of your destination during the flight. As a trainee grumpy old man, I am in danger of going on about it at length. It's bonkers, it's crazy, it's… sorry… enough. You fly how you want and I will fly how I want. Only on the vanishingly rare occasions I have been upgraded to business class, will the system help – well, a little. Being able to plug

Chapter Fourteen

in a laptop computer so that it remains active throughout the flight, rather than having its battery dying in the middle of something, helps and, in my experience, if you ask the cabin staff nicely they will serve you a tiny snack instead of the "dinner-at-breakfast-time" meal, and they actually seem to delight in bringing me the endless cups of tea that help me convert back to home time, though their puzzlement is still always evident. Their constant checking up – "Are you sure I cannot get you something to eat?" – means having more interaction with them.

On one of the rare occasions when I have found myself upgraded, there were only five people in the whole of business class and the service surpassed itself. In one idle moment I asked the stewardess if she was married, fully intending that when she said yes, as I was sure she would, I could say what a shame that was as taking her home and having this sort of service every day would be great. A bit of a humorous way of saying thank you was all that was intended, albeit somewhat contrived. In my defence I would remind you that I had 12 hours to while away. To my chagrin, she said "No". I struggled in embarrassment to explain what I was aiming to say. She may have thought me an idiot, but she just smiled and was back regularly to suggest I ate something having refused the meal.

There is an old Chinese proverb, which says, "He who returns from a journey is not the same as he who left". I am certainly convinced that this is true; what is more, if you choose wisely and pick the right destination then, if life was in danger of getting you down before, you can return with a smile on your face. I think I have done so every single time I have been to Thailand; I am always pleased to have been there and uplifted by my experiences large and small along the way. I am very happy to embrace Dr Seuss's remark, quoted at the start of the book: "Don't cry because it's over, smile because it happened" – indeed it gave me my title.

There is much to enjoy about Thailand. Of course some people are poor, though not in the way of countries like India, and there is a degree of bureaucracy, crime and difficulties of various sorts just like anywhere else, but I love the people, their welcoming nature and pride in their country. I love the look of the place, the architecture and especially the soaring roofs and towering temples. I love seeing monks, shops on wheels and the occasional elephant in the streets. I love the colours and fabrics, especially the rich tones of their silk. I love the smells of everything from lemongrass to spices. I love the food, well maybe not the spiciest, and how meals are served. I love the chaos of many situations and yet the pragmatic approach that does actually get things done, albeit in some cases eventually; I even find the Thais' relaxed attitude to time rather appealing. I love the climate, though the heat can be overwhelming on occasions, and the rain too, even when it is not disrupting something important or flooding half the country. If the people can live with the peculiar political stalemate, one that periodically erupts into discontent or worse, then I can tolerate that too and also the traffic about which you just have to adopt a philosophical attitude.

But there is one overriding factor, so finally let me mention again the Thai word *sanuk*, which is usually translated simply as "fun", though remember it has a much deeper meaning: I love the Thais' laid back attitude to life and the enjoyment they take in the moment for no better

Chapter Fourteen

reason than it is pleasurable so to do. Samuel Butler once described someone as having been "up the Nile as far as the first crocodile". You do need to get into a place and, in the land of smiles, once you do so there is, in my view, nowhere in which enjoying the time spent there is more fun – and there is so much here to bring a smile to anyone's face.

Often visitors are asked, "First time in Thailand?" No. And, "You like Thailand?" Yes. "You will come back?" Yes, again. Yes please; a very big yes please.

ACKNOWLEDGEMENTS

I have met many people in Thailand over the years, some fleetingly, some less so, some in a way that has prompted friendships, and all have influenced this book. I will not, indeed cannot, list them all here, but all deserve a thank you however briefly we may have crossed paths.

Some I have been involved with wearing a business hat (my management training work has taken me to Thailand as well as other parts of South East Asia); some of those have become friends, like Kwai Fun Wong who has worked as a manager at the Tawana Hotel in Bangkok since my very first visit out east. More recently we have stayed regularly at the small hotel *Baan Talay Doa* in Hua Hin and I would count *Khun* Udom, his family and staff as friends too; thank you for some happy times.

In addition, three people deserve special mention for prompting the regularity of my visits and enhancing their enjoyment. One may have all sorts of friends, but holidaying with friends always needs careful thought and does not, it must be acknowledged, always work. But Silvia and Jack, who my wife and I first met on holiday in Hua Hin, have both become special friends and make ideal holiday companions. Our regular get-togethers have been instrumental in increasing the time I have spent in Thailand. Our Thai friend, Siripan Akvanich, and her family, have also been a major influence on our returning regularly: she is a special friend, an unsurpassed guide and, in her own words, "charming too". She also confirms the accuracy of Thailand being called the land of smiles; certainly meeting her always brings a smile to my face. Her cookbook, mentioned in these pages, was published in the spring of 2012; if you are the least bit interested in Thai food do get a copy (*Everyday Thai Cooking* is published by Spring Hill).

Thanks again to Anna Nash at Orient-Express for all her help in making the train trip in Chapter 12 possible. It should be noted also that every member of staff who helped and looked after us on that trip was both professional and delightful: thank you all.

Also, not to be forgotten, many thanks to Sue too – if you had not shared my love of this country none of this might have happened – and your (patient) support of all my writing endeavours is always much appreciated, even when I (rudely?) demand not to be interrupted.

ABOUT THE AUTHOR

Patrick Forsyth has worked for many years as a business consultant and management trainer. Linked to this, he is the author of innumerable articles and a long list of successful business and management, personal development, self-help and career books (for example, *Successful Time Management* published by Kogan Page).

In recent years his writing has expanded into broader areas. He has had a humorous book published about life in the office jungle, *Surviving Office Politics* (Marshall Cavendish) and, more recently, *Empty When Half Full*, a book that highlights and castigates unfortunate consumer messages and has been described as "hilarious". This is published by Bookshaker. In addition, he has had short stories published and also writes about writing for *Writing Magazine* for which he pens a monthly column.

He first travelled to South East Asia more than 25 years ago, and has visited regularly – especially to Singapore, Malaysia and Thailand – for both work and pleasure ever since. His other books of travel writing are: *First Class At Last!* – a light-hearted account of a journey on the Eastern & Oriental Express, the luxury train that runs from Singapore to Bangkok. This was well reviewed, one reviewer calling it "...lively, witty and wry". Another travel title is *Beguiling Burma*, which has a timely focus on a fascinating country increasingly in the news.

He lives in the United Kingdom, in Maldon in North Essex, where he writes looking out over the River Blackwater.

ALSO BY PATRICK FORSYTH

First Class At Last! Contrasting budget and first class travel and taking the luxury Eastern & Oriental Express from Singapore to Bangkok.

Beguiling Burma A lively and light-hearted account of Patrick's journey to Mandalay where he encounters taxis pulled by oxen; rings the largest bell in the world; learns how to wear a skirt; and why florescent pink tiles are used in temples.

Empty When Half Full A hilarious review of poor communication – from the unintentionally funny to the downright devious – that seems to come with every purchase.

www.ingramcontent.com/pod-product-compliance
Lightning Source LLC
Chambersburg PA
CBHW070141100426
42743CB00013B/2792